The Book of Hopes and Dreams

£2.

A Limited First Edition of 250 Copies

of which this is number: 241

The Book of
Hopes and Dreams

Edited by

Dee Rimbaud

Published by bluechrome publishing 2006

2 4 6 8 10 9 7 5 3 1

Copyright © bluechrome publishing 2006
All work contained within this anthology remains in the copyright of
the individual author
Cover design based on a photograph © Dee Rimbaud

The contributors have asserted their right under the Copyright,
Designs and Patents Act 1988 to be identified as the author of their
work

First published in Great Britain in 2006 by
bluechrome publishing
PO Box 109,
Portishead, Bristol. BS20 7ZJ

www.bluechrome.co.uk
A CIP catalogue record for this book is available from the British
Library

ISBN 1-904781-89-6

To find out more about Dee Rimbaud, his artwork and writing visit
www.thunderburst.co.uk

Introduction

Sometimes it's easy to forget just how blessed we are in this small segment of planet Earth that we think of as The First World. Often we become consumed with anxieties that in the grand scheme of things are actually trivial; and in our anxiety, it is too easy to forget those who really have something to be concerned about.

Few of us really have anything serious to fear. Most of us know that tomorrow we'll have enough to eat; we'll have clean water to drink; adequate clothing and decent shelter; and should we ever have the misfortune to fall ill we know that we'll have access to health care provision.

Not everyone is quite so lucky. The people of Afghanistan, for instance, have suffered from over a quarter of a century of invasions and civil wars, which have left the infrastructure of their country in tatters. The Baglan Province of North Eastern Afghanistan, where half a million people live in isolated villages, has been particularly badly struck.

Spirit Aid - a Glasgow-based charity, run entirely by volunteers - has been working tirelessly to bring much-needed help to the villagers of Baglan Province. Of particular concern has been the lack of medical facilities and personnel in the region.

Since the end of 2004 Spirit Aid has been operating a mobile clinic in the region. The clinic - staffed with a doctor, nurse, driver and guard - has now examined and treated approximately 50,000 people.

In order to provide basic medical cover in the region, many more mobile clinics are needed.

This anthology has been compiled in order to raise funds for Spirit Aid, to help them to expand the medical services they provide for the people of Baglan Province.

The Book Of Hopes And Dreams has been in the making for three years. Its aim is to provide hopes and dreams, not just to the people of Baglan, but to you, the reader. The poetry selected for inclusion in this anthology has been chosen for its power to lift you above the clouds, to show you the brightest of visions, to fill you with hopes and dreams. I hope, that like me, you will dream of a better world; and that you will do your little bit to help that dream come true.

My thanks go to the many hundreds of people who have supported this project over the last three years, especially to Michael Burch, Michael Horowitz and Roger Garfitt whose assistance has been invaluable. I'd also like to express my gratitude to all the contributors who donated their work to *The Book Of Hopes And Dreams*.

I hope that you enjoy this book, that it does indeed inspire you to do your bit to make the world a better place. I hope that you feel that the money you spent on this book was well spent... and that you might even consider spending more.

Spirit Aid runs humanitarian projects in many parts of the world. If you would like to find out more about these projects or to make a donation check out their website at www.spiritaid.org.uk

Dee Rimbaud
Glasgow, Scotland. April 2006.

Mission Unstoppable

When the actor David Hayman first visited the mountain villages of Afghanistan, the people were in desperate need of medical care - and hope. As he returns with his charity Spirit Aid, he writes about a personal journey to change lives.

Day one in the main village of the Dahana-I-Ghori district, and the doctors and nurses are already in the mosque, sitting on the floor, each surrounded by at least 20 people thrusting themselves forward for examination. Nearby, the pharmacists sit surrounded by boxes and packs of medicines - everything from penicillin and malaria treatments to multi-vitamins - trying to keep them away from grasping hands.

The mosque measures 20ft by 40, and there must be 150 people in here already. Outside, hundreds more are being kept at bay by Dr Obidi and his assistants, but they are losing the battle. They are swarming past him to force their way in the door, handing screaming babies and children through gaps torn in the plastic sheeting of the windows. Some children are on the roof, trying to find a way in. The noise of shouting and arguing is intense. There is a sense of panic in the air.

The women are being dealt with in another, much smaller, room next door. If anything it is even more intense. Strong men are valiantly trying to hold back the force of desperation trying to flood in. But all you have to do is look into the eyes of these people to know that nothing is going to stop them.

I struggle against the tide to leave the mosque and its teeming courtyard to climb the hill behind. From my vantage point above the chaos, I have a clear view in both directions along the valley. For as far as the eye can see, small family groups of villagers are making their way to the mosque. Out of the houses, out of the caves they come, on foot and donkey, along the well-trodden paths, across the dried river-bed. The women's brightly coloured shawls and scarves stand out in relief against the dun-coloured landscape of this biblical scene. This is crazy, I think. There must be another way to do this. Yet when people are this desperate, there is no other way.

It is early December 2003 and I am three weeks into my third trip to Afghanistan. I am here with £16,000 of aid money raised by my charity Spirit Aid's Children of the Rubble appeal, co-funded by Aid International in Edinburgh. I have put together a medical team of eight doctors, eight nurses, two medical technicians, a dentist, two pharmacists, four drivers and an interpreter, and we are delivering emergency aid to the mountain villages of Baghlan province in north-east Afghanistan; I am also making a documentary film for the BBC about our work.

The people of these mountain villages have not seen a doctor in 24 years, and they are dying. They are stricken with tuberculosis, bronchitis, malaria, whooping cough and gastro-intestinal disease. All of them are treatable - but, in this betrayed and forgotten country, that is not so easy. The life expectancy is 43 years, a quarter of all children are dead by the age of five, and only 17 per cent of people have access to medical services - but not necessarily the money to pay for them.

This country has been bombed and forgotten by the West. Two years after the bombing - carried out by the West to overthrow the fundamentalist Taliban regime following the terror attacks of 9/11 - a little aid is beginning to come in: a few more Bailey bridges over the ravines or some maintenance work on the potholed roads. The humanitarian aid, however, is not forthcoming. The people of this country are dying and we seem to be turning a blind eye. How can we bomb an innocent country, reduce it to rubble and walk away?

Word has spread over the hills to other isolated villages that we are here. A small, middle-aged man walks two miles carrying his 16-year-old daughter in his arms, her limbs badly twisted from polio. "Will the doctors look at my daughter?" he asks, the light of hope in his eyes. "Yes, of course they will," I reply. I ask Anwar, my interpreter, to walk him and his daughter straight into the women's room for examination, yet I fear he will leave a sad and disappointed man.

Some elders come to me with a boy of eight, Mohammad, who has a lump growing out of his neck the size of a football. His father died three years ago and his mother three days ago. He has four sisters and two brothers; he is the eldest. I take Mohammad to Dr Najeep, the paediatrician on my team. It is Hodgkin's disease; he is also suffering from malaria. I ask Dr Obidi, my medical coordinator and the deputy director of health for Baghlan province, if anything can be done. "Yes, if we can get him to Puli Khumri for special treatment. " I tell him Spirit Aid will pay for his journey to the hospital and for his treatment.

The first time I set eyes on Habiba was in January last year, when I stopped in Derwasaqan - one of 16 villages that go by the collective name of Shekh Jalal - to give the children some oranges. She stood out from the haggle of eager young faces crowded round my Land Rover, hands snatching at the unusual sight of fresh fruit. The children were sick, and Habiba had lost three of her young friends to "the cough" in the ten days before I got there.

"They cough and they die," said Sultan, her father. TB, chronic bronchitis, whooping cough and URI (upper respiratory infection) were widespread among the 5,000 population of the villages. Again, these people had not seen a doctor in 24 years. I had come with £10,000 for humanitarian aid, but was so moved by the plight of these children that I took the decision to put together an emergency medical team.

We were back in the country within three days. Over a period of two weeks the team examined and treated all 5,000 people. As well as the chronic chest infections, we also found malaria, gastro-enteritis and serious diarrhoea. I was left with indelible memories of people clutching little plastic bags of medicines as if they were the greatest gifts anyone could have given them; running off with huge smiles of delight, wearing warm new jumpers and shoes or wellies.

I vowed to come back again.

Afghanistan is a hard country. Life in this mountainous, rugged land would not be easy at the best of times; after 13 years of war with the Soviets, four years of drought and the allied bombing campaign, it is a brutal struggle for survival. According to UN figures, it is the poorest, most desperate country outside Africa. It is also one of the most heavily landmined areas in the world. Yet everywhere I go in this beleaguered land, the courage and the spirit of the people uplift me. People tell me their stories not in anger but in confusion and surprise. When is the aid coming? When will you rebuild what you destroyed? Why has the West deserted us? Their smiles belie the disbelief they must feel.

I first came here because I disagreed so passionately with the West carpet-bombing an innocent country. Let's forget all this rubbish about "smart bombs". Bombs aren't smart: they kill people and destroy roads, bridges, tunnels, schools, hospitals, homes, farmlands and lives. There have been many thousands of civilian deaths since the West began its campaign in 2001. How does that stand up to the statements by George Bush and Tony Blair that they have "nothing against the people of Afghanistan"?

There are still some 12,000 allied troops in Afghanistan, hunting Al Qaeda rebels and the remnants of the Taliban - and, of course, Osama bin Laden. The death toll is still rising.

Driving back into Shekh Jalal in November 2003, then months after I met Habiba, I am apprehensive about what I will find. The climate in these mountain villages reaches from 45°C to -35°C in the winter; the villagers eke out a meagre survival by growing rain-fed mountain wheat and keeping chickens and goats. This is my third visit in 16 months, but I am very aware that whatever work I do on behalf of Spirit Aid and our donors is but a sticking-plaster on one of the wounds of the world. Important, yes - but still a sticking-plaster. I will feel happier when we have raised the money to provide a permanent mobile clinic or two, something that can regularly visit these mountain communities so they do not have to wait 24 days, let alone 24 years for medical treatment.

Before I came out on this trip, I wrote to two of the most successful motor dealers in our country, both of them multi-millionaires, asking them to donate a four-wheel-drive vehicle written off against tax, for such a mobile clinic. One of them sent me a cheque for £500. The other didn't bother to reply. I try not to be judgemental of other people's actions or inactions, but at moments like that I want to scream: "Where is your humanity? Where is your compassion? Will one little vehicle that could transform the quality of thousands of vulnerable people's lives make such a huge dent in your personal fortune of many millions that you can't risk it?"

The mud houses range up both slopes of the valley, growing as if out of the earth itself. We drive up the dried-out riverbed - there has been a drought for four years - and I spot a little figure silhouetted on the slope. "Habiba!" I cry. I leap out and run up the hill towards her as she shouts my name. I run with my heart beating to see this seven-year-old princess standing with her adopted brother Bashir. Habiba is alive and well and looking healthy. Her beaming, bright smile and her big dark eyes shine out from beneath a shock of jet-black hair. She is overjoyed to see me again, laughing and clapping her hands in delight.

My interpreter, Anwar, helps with the conversation as I ask how Habiba's family is. "I have lost no friends since you came last. My grandmother is very ill and my father has a ob. "Good and bad news for this vulnerable family. Habaiba's grandmother is suffering from TB, while Sultan is working as a policeman, earning $50 a month: a pittance, but also a lifeline to this man. Not only is he is the sole breadwinner for his family of ten; he is the only one in his community of ten families - about 70 people - who earns money. That is why he has recently adopted 13-year-old Bashir, whose parents were killed in the bombing. The people carved caves out of the hillsides, big enough for families and their animals, so they could escape the worst of those brutal attacks from the sky. Bashir's parents were still outside the caves when the bombs fell.

Habiba tells me Sultan is worried about her grandmother. I tell her the doctors are coming back so we will do everything to help. Suddenly she brings her shawl up to cover her mouth and shyly says: "I've still got it, the crystal." She tells me she treasures the little quartz crystal I gave her. "How about you and Bashir coming in the Land Rover to the main village?" I say. They are ecstatic to be in a vehicle for the first time in their lives as we drive to the main mosque to meet the village elders.

In the road that runs through the valley, I meet the leaders of all the villages of Shekh Jalal. A crowd has gathered around us. I tell them I have come to bring back the medical teams and to distribute clothing and shoes for as many people as possible, and I ask for their co-operation, especially in helping control the distribution of clothes and drugs. But the new head of the main village launches into a speech about how I must not film the women, and accuses me of selling footage from our last visit - which we shot without argument - to make money.

I argue that if we do not have film of the women being treated, it will be hard for me to raise more funding back home. All I have with me is a little video camera. I push it and say: "No filming - no doctors." Women might be second-class citizens in this country, but on this project they will not be.

We are surrounded by at least 100 men, the elders to the fore. Women are in hiding behind walls or cowering in doorways; some of the younger girls, however, are closer and bolder, squatting with the boys. Everyone is intently watching us.

"We don't need your help. The last time you came you gave us bad medicines," says the village head, grandly. I let the silence land in the dust. "Dr Noor, the director of health for Baghlan Province, and his deputy, Dr Obidi, bought those medicines for me," I reply. "Both are highly respected men, and they used what medicines were left, after you were all treated, in the hospital in Puli Khumri."

He lets the silence fall. A white-bearded elder speaks quietly. It is a gentle rebuke. "David has come from far away. He has come back twice this year with doctors and medicines and you insult him like this?" The old man turns to me. "We do not want our children to die."

Another elder continues. "We must change. We know the world is changing. Let this man film his work in peace. We respect him and he is the only one who has ever come to our people and offered to help. Our people are less sick because of the work he did earlier this year. We trust and respect him."

Silence. The first elder utters a quiet full stop: "So be it." There is a general nodding of heads and grunting of agreement. We all look to the head man. "So be it," he says - with a hint of defiance. I thank them all and tell them of Spirit Aid's plans to have a relationship with the people of Shekh Jalal and other communities for many years to come; for as long as we can raise funding.

It has been a strange, unsettling yet encouraging meeting. These people lead a simple life and have little contact with the outside world. There is no electricity, so no TV; no money for batteries, so no radio. There is only word of mouth from those that travel to the local markets for trade: and that word is that the world is changing. Sometimes that change drops in the form of bombs from the sky. Sometimes it is blasted from the barrels of guns. On this occasion, I - with my aid and my camera - am part of the change.

When we start work, we discover that the children are not nearly as sick as last time. There is still TB, malaria and chronic bronchitis, but on the whole the people are healthier than when we were here ten months ago. The children give me the warmest greetings possible, running out of the houses with huge smiles on their faces. White men don't come here, but I have played with these kids, clowned with them, connected through fun. They seem stronger - there are not so many runny noses, filthy coughs and open sores. They still wear the welly boots I brought them before, but they are the worse for wear and in desperate need of replacement. They wear thin cotton tops in this freezing but beautiful day where the temperature is reaching a relatively mild -8°C.

Suddenly a group of women are running from a house towards the mosque, shouting for help. Anwar tells me a mother has just given birth and is haemorrhaging badly. I alert some of the team, dragging them from the chaos of the mosque to go to the woman. Maternal mortality rates can be as high as 60 per cent in these mountain villages. After an hour the team re-emerge to say, in their understated way, that they have stopped the bleeding and the mother and child are doing well. I am glad we are here on this day, and appreciate the skill of this experienced team.

Three weeks later, the medical team have been working almost non-stop, but the effort seems to have paid off. We have examined and treated almost all the population, and I have managed to give almost all of them new clothing and shoes - and even to hand out my oranges and to laugh and clown with the children. The work in Shekh Jalal has been difficult and exhausting. Now Dahana-I-Ghori awaits.

I have been frustrated by the lack of order; by my inability to speak the language; by things not moving fast enough; by not having enough time or money to do all the work I want to do here. The pressure has been piled on, but the work has almost always been good-natured, despite its intensity.

The only anger I have seen has come from Sultan, Habiba's father. He was the most difficult person I had to deal with on my last trip too. An angry man, he fought with and made demands of me every inch of the way. He pushed, he pulled, he argued, all on behalf of his desperate people. I have come to respect his passion a great deal - especially in a land where the notion of "Inshallah", or God willing can lead to a quiet acceptance of one's lot.

Sultan is a stern-looking, handsome ex-army commander who at last has a job. "It is good for us all, David. I will make a good policeman. The $50 a month will help a little," he tells me.

"We have had too much of death. Every family in Afghanistan holds the memory of those who have been taken through war or the bombing or disease. We want to live with peace." He spreads his arms out. "Who asks for this?" he says, and I look at the dust, his worn shoes, his freezing children - who look back with quiet eyes, waiting for an answer. What do you conjure up from the deepest parts of your compassion to answer a question like that?

At 38, Sultan will reach his life expectancy if he lives just another five years. His wife could die during her next childbirth or lose the baby - as she did the last one. The children have no shoes other than the remnants of what I left ten months ago, and no warm clothes. Three scrawny chickens peck away at the barren earth.

Sultan's mother has advanced TB. After talking to the doctors, Spirit Aid will provide the complete course of nine months' worth of medicines they prescribe. But they say she will probably not last.

We drive back over the hills to my base at Puli Khumri. Sultan is in the Land Rover too - he wants to be there when I buy the medicines for his mother. I have also made a promise to Habiba: I will buy her a warm jacket. We head for the bazaar, where for $4 I find her a little padded jacket for the hood. Sultan nods a thank you as I tell him: "This is for the princess."

This is my farewell to Sultan: we move on to the villages of Dahana-I-Ghori tomorrow. It is difficult to say goodbye in the busy market. I ask this proud man if there is anything more I can do for him before I leave. He looks at me and says quietly: "Take me to Scotland."

Within his statement is a message: no matter what my life holds for me, no matter how life improves in this country, it will always be a struggle to feed and clothe and protect my family and stay alive. It is too hard. I see the enormity of the task etched in his face.

After Dahana-I-Ghori we are snowed in for three days; we then have to make our way across a white wilderness of two-metre-deep snow to get back to the capital, Kabul. This is my last night before I head, via Dubai and Amsterdam, to Glasgow.

Leaving Afghanistan is always a rush of mixed emotions for me. I love the people of this country, their warmth and hospitality, their resilience, their ingenuity in survival and above all their wicked sense of humour, which can transcend any language barrier. Yet I have a sense of a job unfinished, no matter how successful my mission.

There is so much work to be done in this country that my sticking-plaster seems woefully inadequate.

I climb into bed at midnight. At 1am there is the unmistakable whistle of a rocket, followed by the "crump" of the blast. It feels about half a mile away. Five minutes later a far more powerful blast shatters the freezing night. It is much closer - I reckon it must be two blocks away. I pull the blankets tighter round me. It is a brutal reminder that, for the people of this country, peace could still be a long way off. But the delivery of mobile clinics may not be ... Inshallah.

David Hayman

First published in The Herald Magazine, 17th January 2004; reproduced here with the kind permission of David Hayman.

Contents

Ron Riddell - Love in a Time of War

para Saraycita y los niños de la guerra en Colombia
(for Saraycita and all children affected by war)

In the silent night
sounds of war return
to haunt me in these hills
and I see again the beauty
of the fields, the streets.

I met you there
and woke with you
between the blazing rounds
and held you one brief moment
out of the line of fire.

In this silence of hills
and poppy-scented breeze
you beside me sleeping
again I see the wild fire
an end of all our weeping.

Moniza Alvi - War and Peace on Earth

after Jules Supervielle

The enemy grabbed all the masks and disguised himself
    as anything he liked.
The lovely day, the harvest, a bunch of roses
    suddenly went mad, exploded, bit you to death.
So many of us died that the crowds thronged below the earth
    rather than above it.
Towns and villages knew that they would turn into corpses
    with the speed that a living soul becomes a dead one.
The churches, which the rough hands of the centuries
    had caressed so often,
    fell to the ground suddenly as if in an epileptic fit –
    to rise again as dust on the wind.
The oaks, in their great antiquity,
    took to the air like a flight of swallows.
The war turned priceless jewels to dry powder
    causing everyone to cough and spit blood.
All those in possession of a body
    felt it turning to fog.
And each one tasted his own ashes in his mouth.
But one day people whispered to each other
    Peace has come.
And that seemed so strange they no longer recognised
    their own voices.
Then the murmur repeated itself over and over,
    beating the air awkwardly
    like dove's wings flapping.
Under all the layers of suffering the word 'victory'
    had disappeared from the language.
Gradually the whole earth, still freshly turned over
    by death and the wounded,
    began to sing 'Peace has come' in a hoarse voice.
The cart found its wheels again and the horse its forelegs
    and hind legs for galloping.

The trees found their deeply buried roots, and their sap,
   no longer terrorised, started to flow
   to the furthest twigs.
The church checked its steeple, right to the tip,
   and its foundations stopped debating their chances
   of survival in the bedrock.
The sheep in the meadow disappeared into their wool
   and their profound dullness
   as they'd done throughout time,
And the cows once again gave milk fresh as the new peace.
Life is put back into the people like a sword into a sheath.
Blood no longer seeks out blood
   in a neighbour's stomach,
The enemy's face stops gleaming up close
   like an instrument of torture
   with the gift of speech
The cantata 'Peace has come' echoes round the earth
And the war dead, so as not to be late for
   the humble public holiday
Race down the endless stairs
Rushing slipping falling
In a great silent tumult.
All those cheated of their lives
   gesticulating and grumbling,
   commandeering a place among us
   as quickly as they can
So they can see, with eyes still able to see,
The faces of the living when at last peace returns to
   the earth.

Tony Harrison - 11 September 2001

for Alfie in Cyprus

Turquoise, indigo, the water
I teach my grandson to love,
who now chews his octopus
swirled in oil and oregano
an inch of tentacle gnawed
and another, savouring the strange,
oil dribbles over his belly,
laughing at everything
was at birth not even a kilo,
so premature he only just made it,
and whose little heart racing
I saw slow down the first time
out of his tent in his mother's arms
the monitor's red digits decreasing,
so he needs no lessons in loving the life
he scarcely scraped into,
but today I made a wish
that all the gifts of this morning,
clear comforting water
so joyfully splashed in,
his octopus, *Sprite,*
pomegranate in yoghurt,
at a beach not that far from
British Army manoeuvres,
and wild forest and mountains,
in an island divided
by bankrupt religions
both bred in the desert,
is all Alfie will ever crave
of Paradise.

Mimi Khalvati - The Children

The children are not ours
but the child they might have been
   is in their eyes.
The children live in camps
but the freedom they have seen
   is in their eyes.

The children wear boleros,
beads and kaftans, tribal
   paint and feathers,
sandals in the snow and *hejab*
as white as snow whose sheen
   is in their eyes.

The children stand with younger
children on their hips,
   in their arms.
Like animals at grass,
stopping in a day's routine
   is in their eyes.

The children hold belongings -
pens and notebooks, blankets,
   shoes and saucepans;
their fingers tell us stories
and what these stories mean
   is in their eyes.

The children are like trees,
scarred on limb and branch.
   In Angola, Rwanda,
Brazil and Mozambique,
firelight, burning clean,
   is in their eyes.

The children are not ours
but you, Salgado, have brought them
    this close, this far.
I stand within a hand's-breadth
and the world that lies between
    is in their eyes.

Robert Mezey - Mercy

for Olivia, for Peter

In an orgy of silence the moon rose
And we sat looking up. Then the wind
Swaying the flowers with a gentle force
Broke open its sweetness on our foreheads.

She said a word long since forgotten,
And you listened to the beating of your heart,
And just over the mountain one white cloud
Came lordly in the radiance of the night.

Something always escapes us, but then the air
Was a drug that we three blindly inhaled,
Till we were lost to hunger and suffering
And could not but behold and be beholden.

Mercy, she said. Now I remember.
And we sat quiet, under a listening sky.
For a moment it seemed we held it all in our hands,
Then let it go, and that was the best of all.

Andrew McNeil - Childlike Force

Childlike force is the force of the future,
Always has been,
The ability to keen joy and brilliance in being.

In South Africa in the red cold dust of July,
We walked in the townships,
Children barefoot playing with
The wire trucks on leashes of the same,
They thundered laughter,
 Into our eyes and hearts.

It is this we took back,
Spoke to in our Scottish classrooms-
Not how poor, how sick many were,
But how the platinum and steel bonds,
Of friendship, of family,
Even out did death.

Magi Gibson - I Want. . .

I remember as a child stroking the golden hair
of an ear of barley, or sucking and chewing
a stem of grass, tasting its bitter greenness on my tongue
or clambering up earthbanks, the damp peaty smell,
the dirt beneath my fingernails

now my lawns are manicured
and the smell of new-cut grass
fights with the smells from factories
and traffic fumes

but I want to feel the earth again
to paddle on cold smooth stones
in the shallow streams of childhood dreams
I want to feel the fresh burst of wild raspberry
stain my mouth with purple stolen fruits

I want to come home running late
a stitch in my side
the night air rasping cold in my lungs
to the sound of my mother calling me
from years away

I want to stand at the kitchen sink
the flannel rough and cat's tongue damp
rubbed across my sun kissed face, my grimy neck

I want the warm comfort of flannelette pyjamas,
the cool cotton of sheets, the weight
of woollen blankets and candlewick
I want my mother's hands tucking me in.

But more than this, I want my children
and their children too, to stroke the golden hair
of an ear of barley, to suck on the bitter green
of a blade of grass, to paddle on cold smooth stones
in shallow streams of childhood dreams.

27

Daniele Pantano - Eine Kleine Nachtmusik

My infant son is the moon.
His face with the crescent smile.

Sleep's music renders us equal.

Soon, we shall dance
in the morning
forest of olive trees.

Heather Taylor Johnson - Refugee with Rounded Belly

Touching belly, thinking home,
blaming each kick for this:
a dust-coated country coloured rusty-scabby red,
brittle like memories turned-to-ash if missed-too-much,
peopled white and dotted black and scarred
with the brown of her skin.

What more than the hope of a baby to come
to change a life from this to that?
What but a birth to add to delusions—
a better world
over there
just across the sea
(smile, dream, touching belly).

Eye the men without the hunt who can see only walls,
pity the women with no milk nor meat of the sunken breast,
cry the children who can't remember but still they carry
broken dolls.
This is native soil under fingernails,
tear-stained language on tips of tongues.
This is fueling hope with foetal blood.
What more than this do I await
a better world in eight weeks time?
(Smile, dream, touching belly).

Joanna M. Weston - Pray For The Peace Of The World

a prayer so big
my mouth expels the plea
on a long breath

the letters fracture and tangle
with whales, car-accidents
smoke-stacks, missiles
taking them draggle-tail
down back-wood paths
to a factory gate

hands pick and pulverize
the jumbled capitals
recycle and burn them
into car-doors

drivers notice
a light smell on their hands
lick the taste
and swallow peace with black coffee
before executive meetings
in paneled rooms
where unexpected words
flow from their lips

K. V. Skene - Ours Is The Breath

Later we'll barely remember
the empty steps,
the nights that never sleep.
Love tiptoes through our ever-afters,
so much is said,
so little shown.
There is time, only time between us
and it is limitless,
and space has dimensions
more elastic than a child's imaginings.
Ours is the breath on which tomorrow depends –
what happens happens, leaves
the taste of kisses in our mouths,
the long dark dying. Someday we'll no longer care
where you end
and I begin. The window holds
a weightless moon,
one faint, forensic star
and an instant of illumination, like seeing
the sun slip through embroidered cloud
to enter blue.
This morning the air smells of turtles,
of snails, of uncut grasses
under a midsummer rain
and everything's calm, everything's cool,
everything promises forever
    and ever
    and ever.

In Wells Cathedral there's this ancient clock,
three parts time-machine, one part zodiac.
Every fifteen minutes, knights on horseback
circle and joust, and for six-hundred years

the same poor sucker riding counter-ways
has copped it full in the face with a lance.
To one side, some weird looking guy in a frock
back-heels a bell. Thus the quarter is struck.

It's empty in here, mostly. There's no God
to speak of - some bishops have said as much -
and five quid buys a person a new watch.
But even at night with the great doors locked

chimes sing out, and the sap who was knocked dead
comes cornering home wearing a new head.

Carol Ann Duffy - Prayer

Some days, although we cannot pray, a prayer
utters itself. So, a woman will lift
her head from the sieve of her hands and stare
at the minims sung by a tree, a sudden gift.

Some nights, although we are faithless, the truth
enters our hearts, that small familiar pain;
then a man will stand stock-still, hearing his youth
in the distant Latin chanting of a train.

Pray for us now. Grade I piano scales
console the lodger looking out across
a Midlands town. Then dusk, and someone calls
a child's name as though they named their loss.

Darkness outside. Inside, the radio's prayer -
Rockall. Malin. Dogger. Finisterre.

John Heath-Stubbs - A Bit Of A Tall Order

A bit of a tall order to ask from me
A positive and optimistic poem,
Who am the translator of Giacomo Leopardi
Whose *infinita vanita del tutto* was his final answer.
But I have to admit, each year before spring starts
A mistle-thrush sings not far away
Each new morning and once I woke
To find a grey squirrel fooling about on my window ledge.

Angela Anderson - Destiny's Garden

Fate is a heartless bitch
who points a crooked finger in time
and makes you the son and daughter
of grief and shame

Dream of a better place,
but take heed

For her partner is Pain,
a double-headed devil
who offers up pleasures unknown
to those who never need or bleed

Chaos is the mother of all life

Think twice before paving
a faultless road for your children
They might be delivered to lesser gods,
manmade and mediocre

Grow them in Destiny's garden
where fierce love breaks earth
and turns brave faces
towards the sun

Silvia Kofler - Dangling

Die Seele baumeln lassen
To let the soul dangle
father would say
as he sat
watching the fountain spurt
water onto
the beach pebbles.
She sits next to the fountain,
eyes glued onto
gray pages of a textbook
she scribbles lists with her fountainpen
for tomorrow.
Tomorrow,
she will
dive into
the mist of a gurgling brook
tomorrow
she may
dangle.

Richard Alan Bunch - Again, Love

Green is alive in springtime
Resurrections burst in daffodils.

Yes, love comes again,
The truest fire in winter

With sonnets undreamed
In lilies of genesis

That dares a kind of joy
Essential and luminous.

David Knopfler - Climbing

With clean fists and straight eyes
I climb, face against the wind
stealing life from the mountain
alone above a ruthless sunset
my ears burn, sharp to your voice
my knees to the pitted grip
lessons hid in every tilt and rock.

I seek resilience, to combat
this greatest nemesis, myself
so, when I receive the folding twilight
I may weave dreams for my resurrection
penetrating your firmament
unafraid, essential in your light
purified... animate.

Annie Finch - The Coming Mirrors

My body thickens in a stem
climbing aloud to keep you here.

My belly thickens like a stem,
my belly is tethered by your days.

Come in, come in, my strong darling.
I'm still a pane of airy glass.

My breasts go heavy to meet you here.

My body turns in place of clouds,
I grow like a pane of open glass.

My body is a forest floor
where needles blend to keep you here.
My belly thickens like a stem.

Come in, come in, my last darling,
and let the coming mirrors pass.

Ruth Fainlight - Passenger

Not watching trains pass and dreaming of when
I would become that traveller, glimpsed
inside the carriage flashing past a watching
dreaming child, but being the passenger

staring out at tall apartment blocks
whose stark forms cut against the setting sun
and bars of livid cloud: balconies crowded
with ladders, boxes, washing, dead pot-plants,

into lighted, steamy windows where women
are cooking and men just home from work, shoes
kicked off and sleeves rolled up, are smoking, stretched
exhausted in their sagging, half-bought chairs,

under viaducts where children busy
with private games and errands wheel and call
like birds at dusk: all that urban glamour
of anonymity which makes me suffer

such nostalgia for a life rejected
and denied, makes me want to leave the train,
walk down the street back to my neighbourhood
of launderettes, newsagents, grocery shops,

become again that watching dreaming girl
and this time live it out – one moment only
was enough before a yawning tunnel-
mouth obscured us both, left her behind.

Charles Adés Fishman - For Eve Rutherford

A dream and a prayer

1.

In celebration of life
the planet stayed awake:
men and women broke free
from their blind rush
toward the future

A few took hold
of the moment   and held tight:
they would solace the wounded
warm the homeless   succor
the starving

There were no marching bands,
no flashing lights, no
colored streamers.

Children waited   for their parents
to change back   for the usual
forgetting,

but — in celebration of life —
there was music and dance,
an air of gentleness
that stirred leaves to a deeper
greenness

Flags stilled over the great hive
of embassies   and the song
of peace   quieted
the last hold-outs among
the violent.

2.

Dear Eve, in your eyes
I see the promise
of a new Eden:
not that fall from innocence

into fatal knowing,
but knowledge of love
and a long memory:
on your lips
all the names of the dead
but   in your hands   the spirit
of forgiveness.

May you be bride of life,
sister of history,
mistress of your heart.
And may the earth dream again
under your healing touch.

Vicki Feaver - Glow-worm

Talking about the chemical changes
that make a body in love shine,
or even, for months, immune to illness,
you pick a grub from the lawn
and let it lie on your palm - glowing
like the emerald-burning butt
of a cigarette.
                    (We still haven't touched,
only lain side by side
the half stories of our half lives.)

You call them lightning bugs
from the way the males gather in clouds
and simultaneously flash.
This is the female, fat from a diet
of liquefied snails, at the stage in her cycle
when she hardly eats; when all her energy's
directed to drawing water and oxygen
to a layer of luciferin.
Wingless, wordless,
in a flagrant and luminous bid
to resist the pull to death, she lifts
her shining green abdomen
to signal *yes yes yes.*

Scott Malby - At Hardscrabble Creek

water passes over rocks
whispering of baptismal suffering,
of endless mysteries.
I am unremarkable it seems to say.
Essence of water and blood my destiny.
My hands get dirty.
I am bound by insatiable appetites,
by the unfathomable and dark graffiti
marking with scars my private sanctuaries
and yet, when I was born
the world began again knowing neither
of success or failure but asking
all the questions that really mattered
echoing inside of me: I am not alone.

From hip, bop, punk rock,
lyrical and concrete. Up from New York,
Black Mountain and San Francisco streets
come incantations caught
in the head lights of my own mind
calling for an end to hypocrisy.
Be real, they say. Be honest.
No voice stifled. No cruelty condoned.
No injustice unredeemed.

Oz Hardwick - The Birth of Venus

Because of the sea and the salt on your skin,
the slip of weed on sand, I
bend to the smooth horizon
of your concentration.

White fingers, still
untanned by sun, move
through mesh of past and future, balanced
on the far coast of recent war. Here
on the shore we remember to forget, yet
behind us lie ruins, but
before:

Here is your hair, blown wild,
your breast, welcoming
worlds to come. We
wait for the sun. Like Venus,
you rise from your shell, your body
offering
the promise of peace.

This, indeed, is ours
because of the sun and the salt on your skin.

Catherine Chandler - Aloft

Bird –
that feathered thing –
sings out the buoyant word.

Thrush –
in winter's dregs –
begs music from the hush.

Across
accordant skies –
flies free the albatross.

Dove –
mourn no more –
for hope takes wing with love.

Jackie Wills - The Me Who's A Wish

Let me be the eye,
a lens hanging
from each stalk
in which an ocean waits,
drawn down
from a cloudless sky.
Swimming in me
is the sun, a curve
of undiscovered chants.

Lori Romero - The Kiss

In the middle of our marriage,
we became fog –
clouds unwilling to fly,
and then you put your mouth

on me, and I borrowed the shape
of the sky and left my graven
image on you.

—

Alan Brownjohn - Happiness near Sandefjord

The height-of-summer forests replete with surprise,
The very woodpeckers crying 'God bless our souls!'
- And our surprise, to burst out in the train
To the sunlight of a plain between rainclouds,
A space of streams and rocky villages
- And step down at the village where Herr Rasmusson
Took guests in a cabin bedroom beside the fields
On the Co-op gherkin farm he was manager of.

It was rain all night nevertheless,
But rain as one of the natural sounds
That partners any deep and healing silence,
And never infringes it. It drenched Herr Rasmusson's
Green lake of gherkin plants; but after breakfast
- Of sweet cold fish and onions and tomatoes
And crispbreads and butter and berry jam and coffee -
We sat and talked in English, discussed the gherkins

- And the sun came out! 'This is good, this is good,'
Said Herr Rasmusson. 'Now our chance to take the crop.'
'If it rain too big,' said Mrs Rasmusson,
'All the gherkins grow too fast, and in the wet
We cannot pick them, they grow into- "Marrows"?
The trucks that come to take them will *not* take them,
They are too big, no use collecting them
For the factory bottles.' 'Yes,' said Herr Rasmusson.

'If it rain too small, they not grow up enough
And we sit round lazy, my husband and myself,
My mother - "Mormor" - our son and all our workers,
We play draughts and wait.' 'Yes,' said Herr Rasmusson,
Looking out at the sun. And Mrs Rasmusson:
'The summer started dry, they were too small,
Now it rain too big, it never stop, we drown.'
'But it shine now,' said her husband, 'and we work. You too?'

We put on his recommended gloves because our hands
Would be grazed and torn by the plants, they could draw
    blood,
And we crossed the track to where the great leaves grew,
Sun-stained and -spotted, like huge maple leaves,
Cupping pure liquid ounces of rolling rain
That ran down in oily drops as you bent, and pushed
The undergrowth aside to get at the gherkins
On their prickly stalks of blotting-paper green.

You had to judge: If a gherkin was too large,
You plucked it all the same, but you threw it into
A separate bag for the uncollectables.
And if it was too small, and clung to its flower,
You left it to be picked in two days' time.
You looked for the happy medium, tried to see it
In a bottle of thirty in a downtown bar
- And carried it carefully to a wicker basket.

Where I crouched, the foliage swathed me, soaked my socks,
And my eagerness dragged the plants out of the soil
They had nearly grown out of anyway;
The best part was my cool, fastidious judgement.
When I stood, the sun hit me! Only we three
- My wife, young son and I - were exhausted already,
And easing our backs, a few dozen gherkins only
Having passed through our hands, strained and sore inside the
    gloves.

Herr Rasmusson, Mrs Rasmusson and Mormor,
And their workers old and young in Co-op sweatshirts,
Were away in a working line that had long outstripped us,
And were nearly up by then to the rocky horizon;
They had filled most of Mormor's woven baskets.
In about an hour we only filled one basket,
Though our cautious gherkins were all the proper size.
We stood and smiled, at a task only quarter-done.

We had tickets for the 11.10 to Oslo.
Herr Rasmusson came down from the top of the field:
'It is enough? You have done hard work for us,
You make many bottles!' His generous broad hand
Of thanks and leavetaking wore no protective glove,
His smiling jaw was stubbly with blond prickles.
We strolled away proud and happy in his praises,
Our own ungloved six hands all joined together.

- Except for our two outer hands, which lugged our cases.

Jon Stallworthy - *In the Street of the Fruit Stalls*

Wicks balance flame, a dark dew falls
in the street of the fruit stalls.
Melon, guava, mandarin,
pyramid-piled like cannon balls,
glow red-hot, gold-hot, from within.

Dark children with a coin to spend
enter the lantern's orbit; find
melon, guava, mandarin -
the moon compacted to a rind,
the sun in a pitted skin.

They take it, break it open, let
a gold or silver fountain wet
mouth, fingers, cheek, nose, chin:
radiant as lanterns they forget
the dark street I am standing in.

Elaine Feinstein - Widow's Necklace

Friends try my stories on their teeth or
with a match: are they plastic or amber?

My children say I must have forgotten
how I used to turn to them so very often,

repeating your words and begging reassurance.
Why should I now recall a loving presence?

But so I do: my story as a wife
is threaded on the string of my own life,

and when I touch these beads, I still remember
your warm back as we slept like spoons together.

Maggie Sawkins - Under a Stone

Leaf,
you no longer know
what it means

to be a leaf under a stone.

You've got too used
to the cold slab weight of it.

Absence of light
has turned you
into a wafer of veins

a leafshadow.

One skipping day
a child will come
and kick away the stone.

For a moment
you will lie there,
afraid of your own lightness

afraid of what you've become,

dazed
by the suddenness
of a white winter sun.

David Hill - Interim Conclusions

Do not expect too much.
Do not expect too little.
Do not expect at all.

The only point of making plans
Is the pleasure of watching them go wrong.

Life is too amazing
To ever be perfect.

Life is finite;
Why should happiness be eternal?
Constant will do.

Live in constant expectation.
Stand back and open your eyes,
Expect and accept,
Live and breathe
THIS moment.

Pat Jourdan - *Other Annunciations*

Not the golden primness of Fra Angelico,
his whitewashed corridors, arched roofspan,
glistening angel. No.
She says yes for all female animals,
yes to the push and heave, the racking pain,
yes to birthing and all its trammels,
yes to forever, again and again,
the intricate decimals of reproducing cells.

Annie Finch - Summer Solstice Chant

The sun, rich and open,
stretches and pours on the bloom of our work.

In the center of the new flowers,
a darker wing of flower

points you like a fire.

Point your fire like a flower.

Tricia Torrington - Enjambment

Where was it we first saw them dance
and when? Or did we always have this image
of him in his Sunday suit, his left hand
holding her right clasped close to his heart,
their other hands with fingers wound together,
their heads held close as if they whispered.

Wherever and whenever, it's always to
The Moonlight Serenade, that clarinet
a *leitmotif* of his survival, what it cost
them; and she is always in her home-made
"happy" dress, her auburn hair new permed
in "The Italian Boy". It was an evening do,

but we were there dressed alike one size apart.
First your feet then mine balanced on his as
we parodied their waltz as if he was our handsome prince.
As far back as that we recognised the difference.
They're always waltzing in that happy haze.
And always to The Moonlight Serenade.

Lawrence Sail - Echo

The year's edge can hardly bear
so much pressure, such stark contests −
between the last door slammed on laughter
and starveling silence, between the glow
of soft tallow and mineral starlight,
between flood and drought, between
darkness unparcelled from gaudy wrapping
and the spick dazzle of the ocean mulling
the next version of itself. Small wonder
that we listen out for a birth-cry of joy −
the seamless ongoing, the way it sounds
beyond doubt, singing in its own echo.

Donald Gardner - In The Alder Thicket

Choreography of kingcups
splayed out
as if flung by a hand
across a stretch of meadow by the pool
          where the ducks wait
their turn
      digging deep in their feathers
            for ticks

and further on a coot, white-billed, long-legged
stalking demurely to the pool,
like a Victorian lady with girded drawers.

Two trains cross,
and a runner speeds by.

I'm lost to the world; no,
it's more that, neither sleeping nor waking,
I become the world, feel its slow turn.

(A couple go past,
a woman with headdress
and her husband scolding her.
The ducks make their escape; she
goes off and sits on a bench, head bowed.)

In the first touch of summer you surmise its end –
dusty August, late afternoon,
a heat haze dumbfounds the blue
while thunder peals along the horizon,
like a set of bowling balls,
or a plane circling off course
lost to all runways.

Parched grass.
This is my secret garden,
where I disappear for an afternoon,
yet even here
I feel the city drawing near.
Amsterdam,
spread out behind me like a carpet,
threadbare, the pattern faded, frayed at the edges.

Silence hemmed in by sounds.
Voices of passers-by
distant as voices in a dream.
A plane homing in low to Schiphol airport

and then there is the sound of silence,
that even the shrill piping of insects
or the moorhen's splash as it somersaults,
hardly disturbs.

Roger Garfitt - Snowdrop

Think of it waiting
        the hard weather out
keeping that lilt to
        itself, that tremor
in the close court
        of the bell

Think of the stillness
        in the sober sides
the steadfast silence
        of the meeting house
Quaker heads bowed
        in patience

Think of the lightness
        it has held in trust
that wingbeat of green
        the petticoats show
when the stiff skirts
        lift at last

Andrew Shelley - New Heart

the space of dead writing
the built clods
the old day
the nothing that you say

water fell around me yesterday
in drops of rain-acid
falling grass-cuttings
bulbs of silver

falling water, all around-
raindrops, on my heart's
withered pith-stone, on its
burnt ember of choking coke,

it swelled slightly, cracked open
like a nut, and a smooth, new heart,
folded inside, came to light

dew-down, moist, brown,
shiny conker, linted
horse-chestnut, polished
in lens-cloth, fine-spun
brushed stuff of cotton, and combed
weave of strands, all jewel-smooth

the shells fell away, cupped,
(cusped), and gathered the last rain,
as drips of cold sun-solder
molten ice-magma, liquid ore,
falling all around in electric
white light, rainbright, raining quietly
remaining water

I peeled the skins apart,
I pasted the dark in, tamped it
into the grooves of the scrollwork
as impasto shadows of the light,
patching in and out of the lightwriting

by cool evening the water falling
all around had stopped and the new
fruit of my heart wrinkled already
like soaked fingers, a creased
baby's skull, an old man's head
or the skin around a damp
white wound

while my pain ruckled in on itself,
divided like a cell, folded in sullen puckers
like a brain, like my dimpled knees,
my uxorious chin, my luxurious mouth

I knew a new skin would form its shell,
I knew within the heart life breaks
was a hidden heart, a secret joy, a kernel
and inside that another, stronger still, a core
I had to be pared down to
before I could be happy
before I could be free
and happy and unhappy didn't count

I set the kettle on the stove, I turned down the tv
I watched the still night through the brand new white windows.

Elizabeth Burns - Blues for Annie

Blue has always travelled
back and forth between us:
the package of tissue paper

spilling out petals of larkspur,
the jug on my windowsill,
pressed flowers, postcards

— the etching of the sea, the painted door —
fragments of china, forget-me-nots,
a painting on silk, a packet of seeds

that will grow into love-in-the-mist.
Things made of blue, wrapped in blue,
tied with blue ribbons or wools.

And now I want to send you
all the blue in the world
if it would heal you:

a whole field-full of flax,
the sea on the day of the wedding picnic.
I want to spread a blue sky

cloudless, over you, surround you
with the honey smell of bluebells,
I want to give you indigo

the dyed cloth drying in the wind and sun
and shower you with cornflower sapphires,
star-shaped gentians, the sky of their petals

I want to let you gaze
into a vatful of the glaze
our potter uses on his bowls –

If all this blue could make you well
I'd wash your scarred skin in it,
I'd lay it like a mantle over you

but there are only words, the written
and the spoken, only thoughts and touches,
only these, and gifts of blue.

Lorna Callery - *aurora in the playground*

blue-purple luminescence
northern lights on a southern hemisphere
of hide-and-seek and hop-scotch dreams

*

there are fluffed up pale people
in the sky like white pillows
they go about their daily business
protecting stars from stares
during daylight hours

*

cotton wool candy floss
passes between them
like the milky breaths of snowmen

*

tippety-tip-toes sparkle
upon a plane of the fantastical
as children stampede like buffalo
in pretty dresses
throughout imaginary realms

*

the aurora is born from tiny palms of colour
chalking up the ground
fingers flick around a grey ocean floor
foot-battered by driftwood grown-ups

*

concrete grown warm to a tropical sea
where yellow kite fish weave
between stones and soft skin
spreading effortless rainbows

Jan Oskar Hansen - When Flies Sleep

Closed my eyes and saw a myriad of coloured lights,
bright stars and fading ones; suns from other solar
system, mathematical symbols and crescent moons
endlessly circling, victim of their own perpetual
motions. A chaos where nothing makes sense, yet
there is a hidden logic which escapes me and I'm
drawn to this silent, faraway world's cruel beauty.
The fly that had been standing still on the sideboard,
awoke flapped transparent wings and flew out of
the window. .

Lorraine Sautner - Prelude to a Kiss

Oh, your welcome voice
which streams - all lilac boughs
of dreams deferred, heavy
curled and whispered
in moist waiting.

~

Speak, my Love,
into slumbered silence -
Arouse the soft and petaled void
into small
beaded promises
of tender encircling.
What jeweled unfolding!

~

Yes, sweet Breath,
drape me in a violet crown
of murmured vows;
Adorn this eternal blossoming.
Ascend!

~

Beloved
song of many dawns,
a Prelude begins
which never ceases
from beginning.
See, our kiss has already started
in words
whose fragrant origin
never ends.

Penelope Shuttle - Fear

I drown water
I make ice shiver

I silence silence,
I darken darkness

I dry out the desert
and poison venom

I eclipse the eclipse,
I shock electricity

I execute death
I memorize memory

I pursue pursuit
and ask asking

I question questions
and listen to listening

I set fire on fire,
burn up the sun

I slow down time
and time speeds up

as only he knows how

Margaret Atwood - Interlunar

Darkness waits apart from any occasion for it;
like sorrow it is always available.
This is only one kind,

the kind in which there are stars
above the leaves, brilliant as steel nails
and countless and without regard.

We are walking together
on dead wet leaves in the intermoon
among the looming nocturnal rocks
which would be pinkish grey
in daylight, gnawed and softened
by moss and ferns, which would be green,
in the musty fresh yeast smell
of trees rotting, earth returning
itself to itself

and I take your hand, which is the shape a hand
would be if you existed truly.
I wish to show you the darkness
you are so afraid of.

Trust me. This darkness
is a place you can enter and be
as safe in as you are anywhere;
you can put one foot in front of the other
and believe the sides of your eyes.
Memorize it. You will know it
again in your own time.
When the appearances of things have left you,
you will still have this darkness.
Something of your own you can carry with you.

We have come to the edge:
the lake gives off its hush;
in the outer night there is a barred owl
calling, like a moth
against the ear, from the far shore
which is invisible.
The lake, vast and dimensionless,
doubles everything, the stars,
the boulders, itself, even the darkness
that you can walk so long in
it becomes light.

Elaine Feinstein - Old Poets

To be in their presence once was
a shot of adrenalin. Wrinkled or flaccid,
they still exuded pheromones. They seemed
already immortal, we saw their future glory
around their heads like haloes.

Even to stand in the cemeteries where they lay
gave us a frisson of joy. We were so sure
the words of their poems would last,
and that the next generation
would be equally in love with the past.

Ian Duhig - From The Irish

According to Dinneen, a Gael unsurpassed
in lexicographical enterprise, the Irish
for moon means the white circle in a slice
of half-boiled potato or turnip; a star
is the mark on the forehead of a beast
and the sun is the bottom of a lake, or well.

Well, if I say to you your face
is like a slice of half-boiled turnip,
your hair is the colour of a lake's bottom
and at the centre of each of your eyes
is the mark of the beast, it is because
I want to love you properly, according to Dinneen.

Cyril Dabydeen - Foreign Legions

This is a surfeit, believe me.
I am circumscribed in the desire to traverse
Whole landmarks: this rage in me
As I am scuttled or going beyond.
Now cockeyed because of hibiscus or bougainvillea,
I contain myself with a tropical burning;
This too is belief, as the spirit harks at luminosity,
The sun itself leaping forward in the constancy
Of rain, the slush of fewer days around;
The weather falsifying grass,
The squelch critical as syllogism.

Thrilled by the furore of other days,
Other longings, a strange madness takes over,
The sun a myriad of rivers in the late afternoon--
And how splendid the lakes, alluvium of a kind!

I gather all the selves mirrored in the display
Of green, and one moment is more fragmentary
Than all the others, as water again scuttles,
Displaying ripples like oblivion.

I hold on to a stopped mouth, ear;
I am vanquished for a while as I sit down
At the edge of the forest and talk in tongues
Of silence, mirroring other longings--
Take me, I say, to the butterfly's wings;
The world itself welcomes me as I am because
Of the imagination's leap and spirited blood.

Disaster comes soon after, and I am yet stuck
In one place; I am hailed from afar, standing tall,
Both feet splayed out. Moongazer too I am,
Whirling with shadows, without anxiety--
And let the dreams take over, let the tides
Vanquish all others while I wait
For the time of rebirth far ahead–
The moment's mammoth start.

Ron Riddell - When the Sun Shines

for my son, Pablo Riddell

When the sun
sends a kind wind lowing
and the air is scented
with home-baked bread

the caroling
of a greenfinch
gives voice to the day
and leaves me
in the empty house
full of the light of heaven.

David Radavich - *Opening*

The mouth of
the hibiscus opens

exotic
as a promise,

self almost obscenely
in the world

against the garden fence
perhaps, or outside a library

whose books travel
farther than any beauty

we can reach without suffering,
shipwrecks: being borne

in a wind dried
without spring rain

dazzling even
trashcan and sidewalks,

tongue
pointing out

such bright and bold

possibilities

Juliet Wilson - Alchemy

In a war zone existence, delimited
by snipers, landmines and hostile troops,
a couple fall in love.

Alchemists, they make a home with
scavenged chairs, a broken table, a second-hand bed
and a sense of humour.

They transcend the ordinary, buoy themselves
against the terrible gravity of war
with the feather lightness of joy.

The pull of vestigial wings between their shoulders
lifts them above their troubled town.

Geoffrey Godbert - Letter

For Goolden

Leaves release the words
on the branches of your smile.
The hand is the flower
of your voice laughing.
Birds carry you high.
The trees are swaying.
On whitewashed paper
I send you the sun
from the risks in the sky.
Its two red lips meet
in the stroke of your mouth,
on the cross of your love.
Black as ink, a moon
brushes this heart line.
There is the eclipse,
close as collision;
sealed in an envelope.

Jay Ramsay - These Days

How are we going to break
the rule of fear ?

Torturers are at it
everywhere

Worker bees and fools deny
the chains that bind
and squeeze us dry

We have no time, no time, no time

And no faith
only in our own creation

In the heart we constrain
before it shakes us open—

Even as we long to be broken,
and return like a river to the sea...

So teach us life
and to breathe again, believe again

That only the best in us
can survive

aspiring to its inward source

No hand of force
can make us dare
the bravest we can be

Only the spirit
that came in freedom

And only the love that knows
that this is its day, life, moment

among all the barren stars
to blaze its name.

Dee Rimbaud - Children Of The Raves

I don't care if tomorrow we cannot share a syllable,
tonight I love you brother - I see God in your eyes
and man, he is good and great! Tonight the hills
are a giant black duvet and everything is safe and
sweet as houses.

And I don't care if tomorrow is bad or sad
or mad and dangerous - tonight the strobe lights
are full of angels and we are all winged children
with sparkly, big eyes full of treasure...

We're like pirates off on a grand adventure,
sailing a polychrome ocean in a polystyrene yacht,
moving to spirals of twisted moonlight,
making harbours of heaven in this faraway place.

Tonight Dan, I'm going to be Peter Pan
and this beanstalk is going to take us up to nirvana.

This is why I'm risking my brain. *This* is why
we are all playing with our bio-chemistry;
snatching brief, lucid, luminous moments
of ecstasy.

It's too good, being a child again;
and no parents around to screw it all up
with their big black book of thou shalt nots.

Tonight Tom, I know you were right:
really, it is never too late
to have a happy childhood.

Maurice Cox   - See!

Wide-eyed I came into this world of wonder.
Wide-eyed I watched the carnival go by.
Wide-eyed I lay and listened to the thunder.
Wide-eyed I wept and waited for an answer.
Wide-eyed I slept … They tell me that I died.
So be it! In my dream I am a dancer
and I dance on, awake, aware - wide-eyed.

K.V. Skene - Bliss

Take off,
face the blue wind,
flaunt your new wings
above a stale world.

Fly high,
split clouds, scratch polished sky,
tear into tomorrow,
chase shadows till you

break through
before the sun. Behind
you roars the bloody dawn,
cheering you on.

Michael Henry - Dream Catcher

My brother is big on dream.
He's taken to dropping the 's'
the way big game-hunters pluralise
elephant, lion, rhino.

He records his dreams in the small hours,
drawing copulating couples
or pianos on a removal truck
playing tunes to change the traffic lights.

I only dream what it says on the packet:
getting lost on the way to the doctor's,
being kept in after school.
I shred my dreams when I get up.

But in my imagination
I can jump-cut
from King George's Hanover
to Patrick Hamilton's seedy Hangover Square.

I could never walk a mile
in my brother's seven-league boots.
I can only hold onto the tail of his coat,
in my laddered socks.

Doug Draime - Finishing Touch

There is a sound
ringing in my bones.
An endless movement
of enchantment and wonder.
The words falling
on the paper
like a stammering Moses.
I hold it in my heart
for this moment eternal.
But each time
a discovery anew,
clapping like thunder over parched
landscape.
Never
a betrayal,
not a false word uttered.
It sends
crippled men
climbing
to the tops of mountains,
climbing
to the sky.
Even in the
stormy, cloudy fragments,
there is
power enough
to pull the earth from its orbit.

Anne McCrady - *Having Invited Him into My Kitchen*

How do you know
what is enough?
the boy asks me
as I offer him a cup
of water while his father works
in my garden,
since it is obvious
to both of us
that I am awash
in *enough*.
His honesty fills my ears
like water at the deep end
of the swimming pool
when I was little
and sat on the bottom
speaking nonsense
in bubbles.
My answer to him is garbled
in drowning words
as I try to explain
my affluence
using soggy excuses
like *comfortable*
and *blessed*.
He isn't listening;
his jaw is stiff
as a diving board.
I hold my breath
as he picks up a plate,
measures its mass,
glances at a stack of them.
When he sets it down
on the edge of my world,
he tells me how strange it is
that I have so many
when I can only use one
at a time

Jack Granath - Student of Munenori

The gray-eyed young candidate
Sat by the water,
Legs crossed beneath him and
Back straight as steel.

First, you must cut your hair,
Whined the priest softly,
A question of discipline.
This the reply:

Only a fool would be
Willing to part with
Gifts of such gamesomeness,
Feet, head, or hands.

True, came the answer, but
Hair has no purpose,
It hangs from us uselessly,
Best for young girls.

Evening was coming on,
Leading its comrades,
Russet-clad thunderclouds,
Stumbling, half-drunk.

The two speakers listened as,
Deep in the distance,
A first and faint grumbling
Tested the sky.

After a moment, the
Boy made his answer:
It does have a purpose, it
Blows in the wind.

Jim Boring - Place, Love, Duty

She should not sit in sadness
Muscles lax about her mouth
Looking inward toward that place
Where fretful hope and passion
Argue, knuckles down, points lost
or gained

Her place, her love, her duty
Her livelihood of caring
Fell full to her from heaven
Caught firm in her wounded heart
Grew strong on tattered blessings
and sang.

Rupert M Loydell - Journey of the Sun Boat

The journey of the sun boat never begins.
It has been delayed by the sale of a house,
a joyrider crashing into our car
and the eternal problem of original sin.

Maybe we'll be blown all the way to heaven
and learn to look seagulls in the eye?
Turning the afterlife into an adventure
changes more than a person's resolution.

A hundred boots are laid out on the beach,
all looking for somewhere to walk to.
But I know I've already been there;
this playful voyage never stops.

(from *Endlessly Divisible*)

Alasdair Gray - To Tom Leonard

While accepting God as the energy, form and matter of the universe
and believing all religious ideas are partly true, I dislike God being
divided into father, son and holy ghost: a division too human and
masculine, yet also too abstract and theoretical to persuade me.
In October 1999 I was delighted to read about God the tree in a
Penguin book of translations from the poetry of Rilke. Rilke imagined
a sixteenth century Russian monk who speaks of God's Italian branch
having an unusually sunny growth compared with the Russian branch,
which nonetheless has its own unique growths.
That brought to mind Scotland and Tom Leonard.

On God the Tree's Scottish branch new buds grow,
proving it's no dead stick.
You flower and fruit,
drop seeds that take root.

Author Note:
In the first version of this poem (published 2000 by Morag McAlpine) the
second line was:

   The blighted prove it is no dead stick,

but a gardener told me that a blighted branch was a completely dead stick,
hence the new version above.

Tom Leonard - *Myths In These Parts (2)*

He'll come down the chimney
once a year and put presents

under the tree. Then he'll have
a bite to eat, before going off

back across the sky
in a big sleigh driving his reindeer.

When you waken up
it will be the middle of the night,

you'll charge through to the room
see your stuff lying there

and you'll shout: Santa's been!

Edwin Morgan - Trio

Coming up Buchanan Street, quickly, on a sharp winter evening
a young man and two girls, under the Christmas lights -
The young man carries a new guitar in his arms,
the girl on the inside carries a very young baby,
and the girl on the outside carries a chihuahua.
And the three of them are laughing, their breath rises
in a cloud of happiness, and as they pass
the boy says, "Wait till he sees this but!"
The chihuahua has a tiny Royal Stewart tartan coat like a
    teapot holder,
the baby in its white shawl is all bright eyes and mouth
    like favours in a fresh sweet cake,
the guitar swells out under its milky plastic cover, tied
    at the neck with silver tinsel tape and a brisk sprig
    of mistletoe.
Orphean sprig! Melting baby! Warm chihuahua!
The vale of tears is powerless before you.
Whether Christ is born, or is not born, you
put paid to fate, it abdicates
               under the Christmas lights.
Monsters of the year
go blank, are scattered back,
can't bear this march of three.

- And the three have passed, vanished in the crowd
(yet not vanished, for in their arms they wind
the life of men and beasts, and music,
laughter ringing them round like a guard)
at the end of this winter's day.

Rasma Haidri - Cabrini-Green Housing Project, Chicago

Tonight
in the high-rise windows
Christmas lights
flicker.
Red, green, white,
shapes almost familiar:
wobbly trees
crooked rectangles
like a child's drawing of a house.

Lights flash on
then off –
each window
a door of stars
appearing
then disappearing
in the muted sky.

On the street below
youths
stand in clusters
loose jackets
lifting
in the chill wind.

Inside
the small ones
look like all children
asleep:
heavy cheeks
soft open mouths.

Lights of Christmas
blink
over their dreaming faces
I'm here, I'm gone,
I'm here...

Kerry Hardie - February Snow

The fields are mud.
The first buds on the ash-trees
blacken to spear-points: stubby, stubbornly raised.

The mountains, ink-blue on their lower slopes,
stand in white silence on a sky
grown passionate with snow-cloud.

Strange visitors,
come to us out of marvellous lands,
proud with a great, still pride.

Rochelle Ratner - Forever

Man. Woman. Birth. Death. Infinity. She watches Ben Casey reruns faithfully, goes to third grade, does her arithmetic homework, on winter weekends goes ice skating and learns to skate in figure eights, her favorite. She almost, but not quite, knows her eight times table, and plays with an eight-inch Ginny doll who has blonde hair and, like her, turned eight six months ago. Other than that, she's a quiet child. The sort of little girl who'll grow up to wear subdued colors and love to lie back, close her eyes, and see bright reds, greens, or purples flowing up and down her legs, skating figure eights in her pelvis, always eights lying on their backs, steadfast and moving at the same time. She wants to believe this will last forever.

Clare E. Potter - Turning Thirty

No ordinary bouquet
from her, a wild bunch
jutting out of the milk jug
refusing arrangement.

Purples tease reds
vying for attention,
pink whispers in between
bringing fighting flowers to agreement.

And one orange
a trick
miniature flowers inside force
the eye deeper, force
my little finger to pry
the flower's flowers to find the heart
—a sea anemone

an ocean on stems.
The red brain flower
a lump of bleeding coral
fits in my cupped palm.

The lamb's tail spray
looks like fox gloves dressed sultry
for the night.
And a pointy green star
pokes out limbs like a trapped beetle.
From the center, face down, petals emerge
fold over like the wings
of a butterfly gathering strength
to push through her chrysalis
—any moment now.

My nail traces under
tight casing
the placenta cracks open
like popped corn

and I see a flower born

Myra Schneider - August Morning

Empress of the back door,
flinging it wide to a garden furred
with minute drops. Pulling off sleep,
its stickiness. Tipping raspberries

into a bowl, fingers sweetened
with pink blood. Out to the park
before mist that's crept from the stream,
thins into dream, before heat and light

are a trap. No dressing-gown here,
no cockatoos. Every blade, every
willow and hawthorn leaf is quiet.
The house - even my rucked night -

could be in another continent.
Wet grass creeps into my socks
and I spread my arms to the silky air,
am five again, telling myself to fly.

Already the dangerous egg of sun
is hatching but I want to stay
with this pale luminosity, with pockets
of dark in the brambled copse

where bats are folded all day
and layers decaying underfoot conceal
cocoons. I'm fumbling for sunglasses
when the oak tree at the wood's edge

cuts out the blinding amber disc.
Branches radiate shafts as if
honey-softened light held in the hub
of roots, had flowed up the trunk

and out through every twig, leaf.
Let me keep this tree, its halo
of rays, and even on skyhidden days
see its divinity within myself.

Carolyn Finlay - Rain Words

Tight shine.
The blue earth moves.

This is mine,
this black branch of morning,
the shine of tight sky,
rain words,
kisses me.

This is gathered-here morning
unlocked in my chest,
stepping,
the scent of hopeful.

This is all
dream and plans couched in velvet
whispers of the Risorgimento,
a padded jewelled doublet,
a conceptual herb garden.

This is my bundle where wonder
and all dreams rise up from new
turning and fragments
of brick and coal and ash,

this is my morning tight shine wonder dream

Bohdan Yuri - A Thought

amidst a cluster of greys,
dark, yet unlike night's call,
brushed, as if blindly,
against the blue green
sea of universe,

a thought,
sparked
in aspiration,

stretching forth
to glow
in abundant glory
and at once in praise
to the light that
gave us here,
between two worlds,
this lifelong gift:

hope,

an unfolding lullaby
for the soul.

Jeanne Macdonald - *I Love A Lassie*

Father buckles the straps on my kilt,
and fastens the leather buttons
on my green wool jacket.

Pushing my hands into the gloves
I admire the stitching, thumbs up
celebrating my fifth birthday.

I sniff them. Count the fingers.
They smell of the front room,
his hide armchair.

The beret is pulled down to my ears,
the feathers, he explains, a cockade
which I will wear for him.

He stands me on the dining table,
tells me I am a true wee Jeannie,
and begins to sing.

Michael R. Burch - Learning to Fly

We are learning to fly
every day . . .

learning to fly–
away, away . . .

O, love is not in the ephemeral flight,
but love, Love! is our destination –

graced land of eternal sunrise, radiant beyond night!
Let us bear one another up in our vast migration.

Arthur Joyce - Métis Prayer

for Dawn Scott

I am half of nothing
and all of everything there is
on Earth. When Crow was born
and fell from the starry lap
of the Great Makers,
I was there.

When fox and eagle
and all the clans
of forest and field
spoke the one language
I walked with them in silence
and understood.

The red ore of these cliffs
runs with the salmon
in the streams of my blood,
and prairie grasses whisper
in the shadows
of my long dark hair.

My people moved
across the Mother's face
with the green grace
of caterpillar on a leaf.
The brothers and sisters
of spirit

huddle their bodies of smoke
around our campfire
and fear is a mad cousin
we honour but will not obey.
Pain haunts us—
a pale scar tearing

across twilight skies.
You can read its history
in the meadows of our eyes.
And when the Makers
return, we will beat the drum
and dance,

we will lay down
and kiss the soil
of our ancient birth;
We will sing the joyful chant
of all Creation made new—
I am, I am, I am.

Rose Flint - Spirit Paths

And what I hope for every winter is to find a way through
to the other side where the jubilant light begins again
in a hesitation of birdsong.

I am learning to see in the dark, recognise that *this is a sign*
and this, these sudden sensual chances and clues
- as in melodic fifths on the radio or a rain-diadem,
or the unexpected arrival of white cyclamen in cellophane –
things the body perceives first as elements of light
and offers up to the spirit, so shut in its hole, mole-blind .

And there are the synchronicities that puzzle you
but make me shiver with their meanings: three aligned
heron feathers or the time and thought of meteorites;
I bring them back to you like trophies from a race of joy.

I had always believed I would die young
not making the markers of thirty nor forty-five.
In a way then, this is all extra and more risky than any year,
this precious time of coming-to-knowing.
But even my acceptance of what is, is, can't fully protect me,
Autumn still brings the familiar fear: Winter will be here
and I will be in darkness, groping forward nervously
trying to remember that the black dragons
and dogs of shadowland are guided by dark mothers
carrying secret gifts of pearl – still I'll cry for kinder weather.

This then, is the origin of fear: that the sun will not rise
and there will be no release from the dark. This, set beside
our knowing of how we must wait always for the hour
when we will not go on into the next season.
Like a film of ghosts, the family, the quick rivers and flowers,
the music and horses will stream past us
covering the brightening land as we are turned aside
into a strangeness we can only trust.

This morning the air reminded me of the country
where we learned to love each other. I know now
that was not better than this. All our symbols and armoury
all our footsteps and collisions are spirit paths, showing
the way through, complex and simple as the lines
held by my hands, and how I hold love between them.

Fiona Ritchie Walker - Interpreting Sand

They travelled for miles, long days and nights
to bring their daughter. Camping by the lake
their fire flickered gold on the shore, spiced oils,
bruised petals, mint tea perfuming the breeze.

Maya's mother draped silk between bushes, poured
scented water over her daughter's shoulders.
A makeshift raft carried the girl to the island.
Waving goodbye, her father saw only shadows,

blurred movements as she made a bed
on the beach, spread soft cotton on sand,
found pebbles to secure edges. She became
dark foetal curves; shallow, sleepy breathing.

Across the water, her mother longed to know
how and when her only child would marry,
her father whispered prayers for healing,
his daughter's face at peace, stilled limbs.

Before the sun rose they crossed the water,
put coins in the hand of the hooded figure,
followed as he read the dips and hollows,
declared the fits departed.

Back home there are celebrations. Maya waits to meet
her future husband. Some nights she dreams
of him, what they will do in the darkness. Always
his face is hidden. Their bed cotton, on sand.

Julie Kane - 15 March 2003

"Beware the Ides of March," a seer said
to Caesar, back when death was hand-to-hand:
this year, two hundred thousand U.S. troops
camped on Kuwaiti and Saudi sand,
each with a dog tag tucked in a boot
and a belt-packed, camouflage poncho/shroud—
and still you breathe the fluid in and out,
preparing to breathe air just months from now.
No blood relation, though you grow inside
my sister's womb, and she and I share genes,
as much the product of technology
as laser-guided bombs and M16s,
you pull us toward the future, unborn niece,
as small and fragile as the hope of peace.

Mike Matthews - *The City of Strings*

In the city that cradles the coffee shops,
held in the heat that dances off concrete,
where we dream we are individuals,

We are the notes of the song,
imagined by the one
who ambles between bus stops
along the grey cracked sidewalks
and carries a guitar—silence at its loudest;

We maintain the momentary choruses—our brief encounters.

In the shadows of buildings
blurred by twilight mornings,
by passing buses and shifting footsteps
dragged by sleepy faces,
            compositions of moments
wedge between brick and glass and steel.

Filaments of a strumming string orchestra
vibrate, and the lines between light and the shadows
tune the moments, the prevalent noise, the hollering, the pulsing
        hearts.

In the jackhammer mornings and noons,
faces in coffee cup steam,
blank shadows in traffic jams,
        the harmony,

men in suits and green socks
stamp rhythms on sidewalks;
women with folders and lunches
gaze at signs for signals
            to walk again.

"There's no such thing as magic," says a man on a bus
who polishes something smooth, round, and invisible;

And in the glances between passing, heated hearts,
a kiss,
        fire that casts the shadows,
and arms that wrap like spiral galaxies
twisting in the beat-sweat melody.

Ray Succre - A-ceremonial

This turn is turned for brilliance,
and this jump had for outspeaking easy.

The green snake drops from an inkling branch and
wraps around the nape like a drunken sweetheart;
its bite is made between rib-stealing jaws
and its old man sores are beaded with life.

This spin tosses out hands and hair,
a people who may fall onto their wrongs,
and this crawl is crawled for balance,
a witching smoke fallen on people.

I lapse to chairs and dirtynail itch the grime
behind my ears,
and no evil comes in through vents
then out through doors,
and no devil is started or ended,
but still these notions are full strangle and choke
the voluptuous wisdoms of my neighbors.

I adopt
this twirl as on the laid out wheel,
I conduct this arch as over the world.

A.C. Bevan - *The Godsend*

Beloved, I
awaited you,
had faith in you
where others
doubted
your very
existence;
When my
agnostic friends
all turned away
in crisis-ethics,
I consulted my
clairvoyance,
made of your
absence –
presence;
I left
gifts at auspicious
sites by votive
candlelight &
shrine, I quit
& re-quit smoking,
shaved my head,
fasted for Lent
or Ramadan,
went vegan,
vegetarian,
on hunger strike,
I didn't mind
yet still there was
no sign of you;

Then
when my heart was
nearly spent,
when I had made
all the arrangements,
cast off all attachments
& willed myself away,
you came
like a small salvation,
like a calendar messiah,

You came
my sweet hereafter,
like I knew you would

You came

Edwin Morgan - A Festive Come-All-Ye

The bling is on the table
The gong has rung its song
The boy has flyped his trumpet
Blowing Wild and strong
Royals in their coffins
Drum their feet - what's wrong?
Nothing wrong, my hearties
The waiting has been long
But now the feast is sparkling
From every blade and prong
None be feart to swing it
None be blate to bling it
Paint the walls
With waterfalls
And see that skip of battered hopes, just bring it.

Lawrence Ferlinghetti -
Recipe For Happiness In Khabarovsk Or Anyplace

One grand boulevard with trees
with one grand café in sun
with strong black coffee in very small cups

One not necessarily very beautiful
man or woman who loves you

One fine day

Scott Malby - *My Life*

In living with you the surprise of you
makes all things new again,
not as symbol but in palpable form.
Not as a servant but as your lover in flames.

Michael Horovitz - Mating Call

– to you to wit to woo you
gladsome voice like
the lilt and tilting
fluttering of owls
wings upon my eyelids –
fain would i turn within that
flocculent heartbud, heart
curled in heart, breaths
rising falling throbbing
as one within our tree
and there bear fruit perennial
unbeknown to mutant man
too deeply twinèd in each other's fleece
for any beast or baron to find out –
yet ready any springing aperture to pierce
to spread our feathers and bare our breasts
and roam the skies and loot the universe
in love that conquers all
outshining every dark night's terrors
– tree of life in whom we dwell
– spell out your secrets
without end, fluttering your
tender soft caress
– owls' wings
upon the eye

David Constantine - *Elm Seeds*

That summer when there were still enormous elms
The seed of them drifted over the asphalt, dots
Of another life in a wispy carrier
To a wall or kerb. I saw
Your bare toes in a pleasant density of seed.

So strange the casting of seed over the concrete:
Down it comes twirling
On to a surface that cannot foster it
Or parachutes in as delicate as a snowflake
With no better chance. But of all this bounty
Of fruitless offering and arrival
I will always love best the seed of the vanished elms
Some carried to bed in your sandals and in your hair.

Thomas R. Smith - Courage

In memory of Rachel Corrie*

As the American-made
bulldozer lurched toward you,
you knelt, submitted with
perfect courage to the clear

purpose in which you lived.
Hardly more yet than a girl,
your heart shielded you.
You were twenty-three.

Kneeling, you stood the test to
destruction, became the rare
hero in a world deranged
by militant armed fear.

"A regrettable accident."
The pharmacist's house fell.
You couldn't save it any
more than you could save yourself.

You were bulldozed a second
time by the war headlines,
a shell battered in the surf
before the wave of Empire.

Barely a woman, yet stronger
than hate, than death, than earth.
And the rest of us—what
have we done with our courage?

*Rachel Corrie, an American college student, was killed by a "supersized"
bulldozer on March 16, 2003, while trying to block the destruction of
Palestinian homes on the Gaza Strip.

Robert Mezey - I Am Beginning To Hear

a voice in this life I am living
every day every night
never before heard

speaking in languages
made of shifts in the direction of the wind
seeds fallen from an apple
feathers in the dust

there is a flight of arrows or is it light
turning the way things turn
after the sun only at different speeds

brilliant darkness as in the night when there is no moon
I must have known it once

as now
moving easily as a hand
among the fiery lights raining out of space
I know what is said but it is
dark untranslatable

a flower suddenly folding up
and rushing away into its ancient parchments

Acknowledgements

Simon Armitage's *Poetry* previously published in *Tyrannosaurus Rex Versus The Corduroy Kid* (Faber & Faber, 2006)

Margaret Atwood's *Interlunar* is reproduced by kind permission of the author, originally published in *Interlunar* (Oxford University Press, 1984)

Alan Brownjohn's *Happiness Near Sandefjord* previously published in *In The Cruel Arcade* (Sinclair - Stevenson, 1994)

Cyril Dabydeen's *Foreign Legions* previously published in *Imaginary Origins: Selected Poems* (Peepal Tree Press, 2004)

Carol Ann Duffy's *Prayer* is reproduced by kind permission of the author, previously published in *Selected Poems* (Penguin, 1994)

Ian Duhig's *From the Irish* previously published in *The Bradford Count* (Bloodaxe, 1991).

Ruth Fainlight's *Passenger* previously published in *Selected Poems* (Sinclair-Stevenson, 1995)

Vicki Feaver's *Glow Worm* previously published in *The Book Of Blood* (Cape, 2006).

Annie Finch's *Coming Mirrors* and *Summer Solstice Chant* previously published in *Calendars* (Tupelo Press, 2003)

Roger Garfitt's *Snowdrop* first appeared in *The Way You Say The World: a celebration for Anne Stevenson* (Shoestring Press, 2003).

Geoffrey Godbert's *Letter* previously published in *Are You Interested In Tattooing?* (University of Salzburg, 1996)

Alasdair Gray's *To Tom Leonard* previously published in *Sixteen Occasional Poems* (Morag McAlpine, 2000)

Oz Hardick's *Birth Of Venus* previously published in *Reach* (#87, 2004)

Tony Harrison's *11 September 2001* appears by kind permission of Alfie Bowlby.

Michael Horovitz's *Mating Call* previously published in *Worsdsounds & Sightlines: New & Selected Poems* (Sinclair-Stevenson, 1994)

Art Joyce's *Métis Prayer* previously published in *The Charlatans of Paradise* (New Orphic Publishers, Canada, 2005)

Rupert M Loydell's *Journey Of The Sun Boat* first published in *Endlessly Divisible* (Driftwood)

Jeanne Macdonald's *I Love A Lassie* previously published in *White Lies Are Harmless* (Diamond Twig, 2004).

Robert Mezey's *I Am Beginning To Hear* and *Mercy* previously published in *Collected Poems 1952-1999* (University of Arkansas Press), reprinted with author's permission

Edwin Morgan's *Trio* previously published in *Selected Poems* (Carcanet Press 1985)

Clare E Potter's *Turning Thirty* previously published in The Xavier Review.

Lorraine Sautner's *Prelude to a Kiss* previously published in *Kindred Trinity* (TJMF Publishing, 2004)

Maggie Sawkins' *Under a Stone* first published in The Interpreter's House (2001).

Myra Schneider's *August Morning* previously published in *Multiplying The Moon* (Enitharmon, 2004).

Andrew Shelley's *New Heart* previously published in <u>Skald</u> (Issue 16, 2002).

Penelope Shuttle's *Fear* previously published in *Redgrove's Wife* (Bloodaxe, 2006)

Thomas R Smith's *Courage* previously published in *Peace Vigil: Poems For An Election Year (And After)* (Lost Music Press, 2004).

John Stallworthy's *In The Street Of The Fruit Stalls* previously published in *Rounding the Horn: Collected Poems* (Carcanet Press, 1998).

Anne Stevenson's *As I Lay Sleeping* previously published in *Poems 1955-2005* (Bloodaxe Books, 2005)

Biographies of Contributors

Moniza Alvi was born in Pakistan and grew up in Hertfordshire. She has five collections of poetry. The first, *The Country at My Shoulder* (OUP, 1993), was a PBS Recommendation, shortlisted for the T.S. Eliot and the Whitbread poetry prizes, and selected for the New Generation Poets promotion. The most recent is *How the Stone Found Its Voice* (Bloodaxe, 2005). She received a Cholmondeley Award in 2002.

Angela Anderson is an American dancer and journalist born and raised in the Californian Mojave desert. She currently lives with her husband and two sons in Brunswick, Germany, where she choreographs for musical theatre and teaches butoh performance. Her poetry and prose have been published in Rohwedder International Journal of Literature and Art and Writing For Our Lives. Her web site is beebop-n-butoh.com.

Simon Armitage was born in 1963 and lives in West Yorkshire. He has published nine volumes of poetry including *Killing Time* (Faber & Faber, 1999) and *Selected Poems* (Faber & Faber, 2001) His most recent collections are *The Universal Home Doctor* and *Travelling Songs* (Faber & Faber in 2002). He has received numerous awards for his poetry including the Sunday Times Author of the Year, one of the first Forward Prizes and a Lannan Award. He writes for radio, television and film, and is the author of four stage plays, including *Mister Heracles*, a version of the Euripides play *The Madness of Heracles*. His recent dramatisation of *The Odyssey*, commissioned by the BBC, was broadcast on Radio 4 in 2004 and is available through BBC Worldwide. He received an Ivor Novello Award for his song-lyrics in the Channel 4 film Feltham Sings, which also won a BAFTA. His first novel, *Little Green Man*, was published by Penguin in 2001. His second novel *The White Stuff* was published in 2004.

Margaret Atwood is the author of more than forty books of fiction poetry, and critical essays. Her most recent book *Moral Disorder*, a collection of interconnected short stories was published by McClelland & Stewart in Canada and Bloomsbury in the UK, in September 2006. Her novel, *Oryx and Crake*, was short-listed for the Man Booker Prize and the Giller Prize in Canada. Her other books include the 2000 Booker Prize winning, *The Blind Assassin*, *Alias Grace*, which won the Giller Prize in Canada and the Premio Mondello in Italy, *The Robber Bride*, *Cat's Eye*, *The Handmaid's Tale* and *The Penelopiad*. Margaret Atwood lives in Toronto with writer Graeme Gibson.

A C Bevan: poems have appeared in newspapers & magazines in the United Kingdom, Europe & America – most notably in *Poetry Review*, *Poetry Salzburg* & *Caveat Lector* respectively, as well as the anthology: *Bleeding Hearts – Love Poems for the Nervous & Highly Strung* (Aurum Press [UK] / St Martins Press [US]). His first pamphlet collection, *Of Sea Graves and Sand Shrines*, was published by Arc Publications in January 2001 & led to further interest from Channel 4 & BBC Radio. His first full-length collection will be published by Salmon in 2007.

Jim Boring lives on the edge of the Everglades in Margate, Florida, USA. His poetry has appeared in many venues most notably the literary magazine, *Lit Pot*. His most recent manuscript, *Condo and Other Poems*, reflects on the process of aging in a community of the aged.

Alan Brownjohn was born in London on 28 July 1931 and was educated at Merton College, Oxford. He worked as a schoolteacher between 1957 and 1965 and lectured at Battersea College of Education and South Bank Polytechnic until he left to become a full-time freelance writer in 1979. His first collection of poetry, *The Railings*, was published in 1961. Other poetry books include *Collected Poems 1952-1983* (1983) and *The Observation Car* (1990). He is also the author of three novels, as well as two books for children and a critical study of the poet Philip Larkin.

Richard Alan Bunch, born in Honolulu, grew up in the Napa Valley. His poetry works include *Summer Hawk* and *Wading the Russian River*. *Night Blooms* is a selection of journal entries on philosophy, literature, and religion. His stories have appeared in several venues. He is also author of the play, *The Russian River Returns*. His poetry has appeared in *Orbis, Avocet, Poetry New Zealand, Oregon Review, Poetry Nottingham* and the *Hawai'i Review*. His latest poetry collection is *Running for Daybreak* (Mellen Poetry Press).

Michael R. Burch is the editor of *The HyperTexts*, where he has published the work of three Pulitzer Prize nominees and recent winners of the T. S. Eliot, Richard Wilbur and Howard Nemerov awards. His work has appeared over 400 times in literary journals around the globe, including *The Chariton Review, Poetry Magazine, Verse, Poet Lore, Unlikely Stories, Light Quarterly, Writer's Digest – The Year's Best Writing 2003, The Best of the Eclectic Muse 1989-2003, The Lyric, ByLine, Icon* and *Nebo*.

Elizabeth Burns has published two collections of poetry, *Ophelia and other poems* (Polygon, 1991) and *The Gift of Light* (diehard, 2000), and several pamphlets with Galdragon Press. Her work has also been published in anthologies such as *Dream State: The New Scottish Poets* (Polygon, 1994 & 2002), *Atoms of Delight: An Anthology of Scottish Haiku and Short Poems* (Pocketbooks, 2001), *Modern Scottish Women Poets* (Canongate, 2003) and *Handsel: Poems for Births and Baby Namings* (Scottish Poetry Library, 2005).

Lorna Callery is a Glasgow based artist, writer and tutor interested in broadening the boundaries between art forms, specifically visual art and creative writing. Much of Lorna's art is text based, experimenting with concrete poetry within the gallery context in order to challenge the viewer's perceptions of what constitutes a particular art form. Is it visual art/is it poetry? Why do we feel the need to constantly categorise what we have created? For more information contact: polkadotpunks@hotmail.com

Catherine Chandler was born in New York and raised in Pennsylvania. In 1972, she and her husband, Hugo Oliveira, settled in Montreal, Canada, where she lectures in Spanish at McGill University's Department of Translation Studies. Her poems and translations have been published or will soon appear in such journals as *SPSM&H (Amelia)*, *The Lyric*, *Iambs and Trochees*, *Raintown Review*, *Harp-Strings Poetry Journal*, *Blue Unicorn*, *Texas Poetry Journal*, and *Modern Haiku*. Samples of her work can be read at *The HyperTexts* at www.thehypertexts.com under "Contemporary Poets/Artists".

David Constantine has published half a dozen volumes of poetry, most recently a *Collected Poems* (Bloodaxe Books 2004) and a volume of short stories, *Under the Dam* (Comma Press 2005). He is a translator of Hölderlin, Goethe and Brecht. With his wife Helen he edits the magazine *Modern Poetry in Translation*.

Maurice Cox is an author/songsmith whose anthems have been sung throughout the UK, in venues ranging from small folk clubs and civic centres to the Royal Albert Hall (*Holy Day! 2001*, in collaboration with Andrew Campling, founder/musical director of the Dockland Singers). After surviving major surgery for cancer, he now lives in retirement in Fort William in the Scottish Highlands.

Cyril Dabydeen: work has been anthologized in over 20 volumes in seven countries, including in the *Penguin Book of Caribbean Verse* and the *Oxford Book of Caribbean Poetry*. His own recent books include *Imaginary Origins: Selected Poems* (Peepal Tree Press, UK), *Play a Song Somebody: New and Selected Stories* (Mosaic Press, Canada), and the novel *Drums of My Flesh* (TSAR, Canada). He has juried for Canada's Governor General's Award for Poetry, and America's Neustadt International Prize for Literature, and has read across North America, UK and Europe, the Caribbean and Asia. He teaches English at the University of Ottawa, Canada. He was official Poet Laureate of Ottawa (1984-87).

Doug Draime, poet, short story writer and playwright has been writing and publishing since the late 1960's. His most recent books include: *Slaves Of The Harvest* (Indian Heritage Publishing, 2002), *Unoccupied Zone* (Pitchfork Press, 2004), *Spleen* an online book, (Poetic Inhalation, 2005), and forthcoming from Scintillating Publications, *Spiders And Madmen*. Awarded PEN grants in 1987 and 1991. His work has appeared in hundreds of print magazines and online journals. He currently lives in Oregon with his wife, writer Carol Shepherd-Draime.

Carol Ann Duffy, born in Glasgow in 1955, grew up in Stafford and attended university in Liverpool. She lived for several years in London before moving back north again and now lives in Manchester with her young daughter. Her poetry has been critically acclaimed and she has received numerous awards. Her collections include *Standing Female Nude* and *The Other Country*, which both earned her a Scottish Arts Council Award; *Selling Manhattan*, which won a Somerset Maugham Award (1988), a Dylan Thomas Award (1989) and a Cholmondelay Award (1992); *Mean Time*, which won a Scottish Arts Council Book Award, the Forward Prize and the Whitbread Award for Poetry (1993); and *The World's Wife*, which received the E.M. Forster Award in the USA. Since becoming a mother herself, she has also begun to write for children and her collections of poetry for younger readers are entitled *Meeting Midnight* (shortlisted for the Whitbread Children's book of the year in 1999) and *The Oldest Girl In The World* (which received the Signal Prize in 2000). She has also written versions of Grimm's fairy tales and is the editor of several anthologies for both adults and children.

Ian Duhig worked with homeless people for 15 years before becoming a full-time writer and teacher of writing. He has written four books of poetry, the most recent of which - *The Lammas Hireling* (Picador 2003) - was a PBS Choice and shortlisted for the Forward and T.S. Eliot Best Collection Prizes. His next, *The Speed of Dark*, is due from Picador in 2007.

Ruth Fainlight was born in New York City, but has lived in England since the age of 15. She has published thirteen collections of poems in England and the USA, as well as two volumes of short stories. Books of her poems have appeared in Portuguese, French, Spanish and Italian translation. She received the Hawthornden and Cholmondeley Awards in 1994, and her collection, *Sugar-Paper Blue* (Bloodaxe, 1997) was shortlisted for the 1998 Whitbread Award. Her latest collection is *Moon Wheels* (Bloodaxe, 2006).

Vicki Feaver was born in Nottingham in 1943. She studied music at Durham University and later, after bringing up four children, English at University College London. She has published three volumes of poetry, *Close Relatives* (Secker 1981), *The Handless Maiden* (Cape 1994) and *The Book of Blood* (Cape 2006). Previously a professor at the University of Chichester, she moved to Scotland in 2000 and lives with her husband and dog on the edge of the Pentlands.

Elaine Feinstein is a prize-winning poet, novelist and biographer. In 1990, she received a Cholmondeley Award for Poetry, and was given an Honorary D.Litt from the University of Leicester . She is a Fellow of he Royal Society of Literature . Her versions of the poems of Marina Tsvetaeva were first published in 1971, and remain in print from OUP/Carcanet in the UK and Penguin in USA. Her *Collected Poems and Translations* (2002) was a Poetry Book Society Special Commendation. Her web site is at www.ElaineFeinstein.com

Lawrence Ferlinghetti was born in Yonkers in 1919. In 1953 he co-founded, with Peter D. Martin, City Lights, one of the first all-paperbound bookstores in the country, and by 1955 had launched the City Lights publishing house, whose publication of Allen Ginsberg's *Howl* in 1956 led to the publisher's arrest on obscenity charges. In a widely publicized first amendment case, the publishers were vindicated, drawing international attention to San Francisco Renaissance and Beat movement writers. Ferlinghetti is the author of *A Coney Island of the Mind*, one of the most popular poetry books in the U.S., with close to 1,000,000 copies in print. His most recent book is *A Far Rockaway of the Heart*. In August 1998, he was named San Francisco's first Poet Laureate.

Annie Finch is an American poet, translator, librettist, critic and editor. She has published four books of poetry, including *Calendars* (Tupelo, 2003), shortlisted for the Foreword Poetry Book of the Year Award; *The Encyclopaedia of Scotland* (Salt Publishing, 2004), and a translation of the *Complete Poems* of Louise Labé (University of Chicago Press, 2006). Her opera based on the life of Marina Tsvetaeva premiered from American Opera Projects in 2003. Her most recent of several anthologies and books on poetics is *The Body of Poetry: Essays on Women, Form, and the Poetic Self* (Michigan, 2005). She directs the Stonecoast Brief-Residency MFA at the University of Southern Maine, and her website is at www.anniefinch.com

Carolyn Finlay grew up in Australia and came to England in 1969. Her poems have appeared in magazines such as *Terrible Work, Acid Angel, Fire, Outposts*, etc, and in the anthologies *Earth Ascending* (Stride 1995) and *Earth Songs* (Green Books 2002). In her two books of poetry, *Giveaway* (Stride 1996) and *Foreigner* (Waterdog Press 2001), she explores and celebrates our human experience of simultaneous multi-levelled reality. Her short story, 'Zoom', appears in *Necrologue, the Diva Book of the Dead and the Undead* (Diva Books 2003).

Charles Adés Fishman is director of the Distinguished Speakers Program at Farmingdale State University and poetry editor of *New Works Review*. His books include *Mortal Companions, Blood to Remember: American Poets on the Holocaust*, and *The Death Mazurka*, which was nominated for the 1990 Pulitzer Prize in Poetry. His most recent collections are *Country of Memory* (Uccelli Press), and *5,000 Bells* (Cross-Cultural Communications), both 2004. His new book of poems, *Chopin's Piano*, has just been published by Time Being Books, which will publish a revised second edition of *Blood to Remember* in 2007.

Rose Flint, an award winning poet, has three collections *Blue Horse of Morning* (Seren) *Firesigns* (Poetry Salzburg) and *Nekyia* (Stride). She is an art therapist and uses the healing qualities of poetry in her work as Lead Writer for the Kingfisher Project, based in the hospital and community of Salisbury. She teaches creative writing and is a tutor for Arvon and Ty Newydd. Her themes celebrates the sacredness of life, with a sense of spirit and relationship.

Donald Gardner: London-born, lived in New York in the 1960s where he read his poetry with Ginsberg, Corso and others. He has lived in Holland since 1979. He is a translator of poetry, for instance, Octavio Paz's *Sun Stone*. His collection, *How to Get the Most out of Your Jet Lag* appeared in 2001(Ye Olde Font Shoppe, New Haven). His most recent book of poems is *The Glittering Sea* (Hearing Eye, 2006). His translations of the poems of Remco Campert, *I Dreamed in the Cities at Night* have just been published (Arc Publications, 2006). His website is: www.donaldgardner.net

Roger Garfitt is a Royal Literary Fund Fellow at the University of Wales, Swansea, and runs Poetry Masterclasses for the University of Cambridge Institute of Continuing Education at Madingley Hall. He performs Poetry & Jazz with Nikki Iles and the John Williams Septet and Poetry & Dulcimer Music with Sue Harris on the hammered dulcimer. His *Selected Poems* are published by Carcanet and he is completing a memoir, *The Horseman's Word*, for Secker & Warburg.

Magi Gibson has published four collections of poetry. She won the Scotland on Sunday/Women 2000 Writing Prize. Poems in *Scottish Love Poems* and *Modern Scottish Women Poets* (both Canongate), and *The Twentieth Century Book of Scottish Poetry* (Edinburgh University Press). Her third poetry collection, *Wild Women of a Certain Age*, is now in its third print run. She lives in Scotland with partner, comedy writer and stand-up comedian, Ian Macpherson.

Geoffrey Godbert has fourteen collections of poetry, two of essays, a memoir and a treatise. He is co-editor of two Faber poetry anthologies and editor of an anthology of prose poems. His poems are included in a modern ballet. Of his work, Harold Pinter comments: "Geoffrey will certainly end up with the poets in heaven."

Jack Granath lives in Kansas City, Missouri and works in a library in Kansas City, Kansas. His poetry has appeared in *Alaska Quarterly Review* and *The Formalist* among other publications. More information is available at www.jackgranath.com.

Alasdair Gray: born in 1934 and dwelling in Glasgow became jack of several trades being unable to earn a living by one, therefore cannot be taken seriously. He has written plays, novels, stories, verses, literary histories and political pamphlets; has designed and illustrated books, mainly his own; has painted portraits, landscapes, stage scenery and mural decorations. A Life in Pictures, a book about his art, and John Tunnock, another novel will probably be published in 2007. His website is www.alasdairgray.co.uk

Rasma Haidri grew up in the U.S. and currently lives on the arctic seacoast of Norway. Her writing has appeared in literary journals such as *Nimrod*, *Prairie Schooner* and *Fine Madness*; and been widely anthologized, most recently in *Only the Sea Keeps* (Bayeux Arts), and *Waking up American* (Seal Press).

Jan Oscar Hansen: Norwegian poet, published in magazines, collections, in anthologies and on the Internet.

Kerry Hardie: Born 1951, lives in Co. Kilkenny, Ireland. Publications: Poetry *–A Furious Place* (Gallery Press, 1996); *Cry For The Hot Belly* (Gallery Press, 2000); *The Sky Didn't Fall* (Gallery Press, 2003). *The Silence Came Close* forthcoming, 2006. Novels: *Hannie Bennet's Winter Marriage* (Harper Collins 2000); *The Bird Woman* (Harper Collins, July 2006). Many prizes and commendations. Has been awarded residencies in Portugal, Switzerland, Paris, Scotland, Spain. Reviews for the Boston Globe. Her work has been widely anthologised.

Oz Hardwick is a writer, photographer and would-be musician - frequently in combination. He is passionate about poetry, medieval art & literature, and 70s bands most people have forgotten. In order to pay the rent he lectures in English Literature. His most recent collection is *The Kind Ghosts* (bluechrome, 2004) and he edited the anthology, *Truths and Disguises* (bluechrome, 2005).

Tony Harrison was born in Leeds in 1937. His many collections of poems include: *The Loiners* (awarded the Geoffrey Faber memorial Prize in 1972); *Palladas: Poems* (1975); from *The School Of Eloquence* (1981); *Continuous* (1981); *Selected Poems* (Penguin, 1984 second ed. 1987, third ed.1995); v. (Bloodaxe Books, 1985 new enlarged ed. 1989); *The Gaze Of The Gorgon* (Bloodaxe, 1992, awarded Whitbread Prize for Poetry); *The Shadow Of Hiroshima* and other film poems (Faber, 1995, awarded the William Heinemann Prize 1996) and *Laureate's Block And Other Poems* (Penguin, 2000). His most recent collection of poems, *Under The Clock* was published in May 2005 (Penguin Books).

John Heath-Stubbs was born in 1918. He was educated at The Queen's College, Oxford, where his contemporaries were C.S.Lewis and Tolkein. He published his first poems in the wartime volume *Eight Oxford Poets* and has gone on to write poetry, plays and literary essays that ignore fashion. One of the most celebrated poets of his generation, he is noted also for his translations of Middle Eastern poets, his role as teacher to new generations of writers and as a voice keeping the long form poem an active and vibrant tradition. He received the Queen's Gold Medal for Poetry.

Michael Henry lives in Cheltenham. He has had three collections published with Enitharmon, the last of which, "Footnote to History" was published in 2001. He is currently completing a new collection. His poetry also appeared in many anthologies and poetry magazines.

David Hill is a writer, performer and translator of verse; he has contributed to film and theatre productions, national newspapers, poster campaigns, and over 20 anthologies. His live engagements have included literary readings, slams, business and private functions, cabarets and comedy shows in the UK, the US, Austria, Denmark, Holland, Hungary and the Czech Republic. He has also written lyrics for recording artists.

Michael Horovitz is editor-publisher of New Departures, and torchbearer-presenter of Poetry Olympics festivals and Jazz Poetry SuperJams. He has recently formed the William Blake Klezmatrix band, to perform Blake's lyrics and much else in musical settings that range from blues to klezmer and folk-rock to calypso. His books in print include a 670-line rural rhapsody *Midsummer Morning Jog Log*, and *Wordsounds & Sightlines: New & Selected Poems*, as well as the multi-faceted *POW!*, *POP!*, *POM* and *POT!* Anthologies. Contact: New Departures, PO Box 9819, London W11 2GQ, England. Email: info@poetryolympics.com Website: www.poetryolmypics.com

Heather Taylor Johnson moved from America to Australia in 1999 and found a home in Adelaide, South Australia. Along with gaining her permanent residency, a true blue Aussie husband and two children who call her 'mum', she is currently the poetry editor for the literary magazine Wet Ink and is working on the finishing touches to her PhD in Creative Writing at the University of Adelaide. The novel manuscript that transpired as a result of her degree was longlisted for the *Australian/*Vogel Award in 2005.

Pat Jourdan: newest book is *Average Sunday Afternoon*, (Poetry Monthly Press, ISBN 1-905126-29-8). Part of the Galway writing scene for many years. Published *Turpentine* in 2004 (Motet, ISBN 0-9542399-1-1). She is mentioned as "a little-known but gifted poet" by Ian McEwan in the novel "Saturday" (2005).

Arthur Joyce is perhaps best known for his newspaper columns and books on the history of the West Kootenay region of British Columbia, Canada. He has been an organizer of poetry tours and cafés since the '80s, and a frequent performer on the Kootenay literary scene. His poetry and essays on poetics have been published in various Canadian literary journals, including *Canadian Author*, *The Fiddlehead*, *The New Quarterly*, *Whetstone*, *The New Orphic Review*, and *Horsefly*.

Julie Kane, a native of Boston and longtime resident of Louisiana, teaches at Northwestern State University in Natchitoches, Louisiana. Her second full-length poetry collection, *Rhythm & Booze* (University of Illinois Press, 2003) was selected by Maxine Kumin as a winner in the National Poetry Series and was a finalist for the 2005 Poets' Prize. Her poems have appeared in such journals as *The Southern Review, The Antioch Review, Prairie Schooner, London Magazine, Verse Daily, Feminist Studies,* and *The Formalist,* as well as in various anthologies.

Mimi Khalvati was born in Iran. Her Carcanet collections include 'In White Ink' (1991), 'Mirrorwork' (1995), for which she received an Arts Council of England Writers' Award, 'Entries on Light' (1997), 'Selected Poems' (2000) and 'The Chine' (2002). She is the founder of the Poetry School where she teaches and currently holds a Royal Literary Fund Fellowship at City University.

David Knopfler: founder of rock group Dire Straits, he subsequently faithfully pursued his own musical vision, writing and producing his own compositions on nine solo CDs to date. A lifelong member of organizations like Amnesty International, David has always made uncompromising life choices: "I don't regard what I do as remotely glamorous. I write, record and perform my music because I completely love doing it and despite any so called *celebrity status* that sometimes comes with the job." As well as having produced a clutch of underscores for film and TV projects, David's first book of poetry entitled *Blood Stones and Rhythmic Beasts* was released in 2005 by Blackwing Books.

Silvia Kofler was born in Graz, Austria, has lived in London and Paris and moved to Kansas City in 1979. She is editor/publisher of Thorny Locust. Her work has been published in New Letters, Black Moon, Potpourri, The Same (published a version of "Dangling"), The Kansas City Star and numerous other publications. Her book, *From the Suburbs with the Wedding Dress in its Coffin/Vom Vorort mit dem Hochzeitskleid im Sarg*, was published by The Edwin Mellen Press. She is a member of the American Literary Translators Association, and lectures at KU and Rockhurst University.

Rupert M Loydell is Lecturer in Creative Writing at University College Falmouth, Managing Editor of Stride Publications, Editor of *Stride* magazine, and a regular contributor to *Tangents* magazine. Recent publications include *A Conference of Voices*, *The Museum of Light* and *The Smallest Death*, as well as several collaborative books.

Jeanne Macdonald was awarded her MA, Writing Poetry, at the University of Newcastle upon Tyne, 2003. Her first collection, *white lies are harmless*, Diamond Twig, published 2004. She launched Blinking Eye Publishing in 2004, promoting the work of writers over 50, and acknowledges North East Arts Council, England, for financial support. Blinking Eye publishes 2 books each year from the results of an annual poetry competition: overall winner's collection, and an anthology of poems by commended poets.

Scott Malby is a frequent contributor to journals worldwide. His work has been translated into German, French and Italian. He resides in Coos Bay, Oregon, U.S.A.

Mike Matthews lives in Austin, Texas, with his wife, Venus, and his three children: two boys, Jade and Drae, and his four month old daughter, Sophia. He teaches college English classes in Killeen, Texas. He received his MFA in creative writing from Texas State University in San Marcos in 1998, and has since published several poems in journals around the United States and in Scotland. Mike Matthews can be contacted by email: MikDavid@hotmail.com

Anne McCrady is a poet, storyteller and inspirational speaker whose writing appears in journals, anthologies and performances including the Texas Storytelling Festival and the National Storytelling Conference. Her award-winning collection of poems, *Along Greathouse Road*, is available in print (Eakin Press, 2004) and on CD (InSpiritry Productions, 2005) along with her narrative gift book, *Kevin and the Seven Prayers* (InSpiritry Press, 2002). Anne is a Texas Commission on the Arts Touring Artist, a councilor for the Poetry Society of Texas and an assistant editor for Gin Bender Poetry Review. She welcomes visitors to her website, www.InSpiritry.com

Andrew McNeil is a teacher/writer living in Fife. He and his partner have two great kids. He was born in Ohio, USA and soon imbibed Scots and the salty air in the East Neuk of Fife. He was educated at Edinburgh University and Jordanhill College. In work-holed severely by postgraduate studies he dreams and has visions of a Scotland coming to fully esteem itself through any language and dream!

Robert Mezey I was born in Philadephia in 1935 and educated at Kenyon College, the U. of Iowa, and Stanford U. My first book, *The Lovemaker*, won the Lamont and was published in 1961. I have published a number of other volumes of verse, inlcuding *White Blossoms*, *The Door Standing Open* and *Evening Wind*, the most recent being my *Collected Poems* (U. of Arkansas Press, 2000) which won the Poets Prize. I have co-edited (with Donald Justice) the collected poems of Henri Coulette, and I have edited the selected poems of Thomas Hardy, E. A. Robinson and Dick Barnes, and three anthologies, *Naked Poetry*, *Poems From The Hebrew* and *Poems Of The American West*. With Dick Barnes I translated the collected poems of Jorge Luis Borges. I have also been awarded fellowships from the National Endowment for the Arts, the Guggenheim Foundation and the Ingram Merrill Foundation, and a prize from the American Academy of Arts and Letters.

Edwin Morgan was born 27 April 1920 in Glasgow. He began his studies at Glasgow University in 1937. He interrupted his studies in 1940 to join the Royal Army Medical Corps, then returned to university in 1946. He graduated the following year with a First Class Honours Degree, and became lecturer at Glasgow University, turning down a scholarship to Oxford; he took early retirement in 1980. He published numerous volumes of poetry, as well as collections of essays, most of which are available at Carcanet Press and Mariscat Press. His volume of *Collected Poems* (Carcanet Press, 1990) is the largest, a very wide ranging collection. He was announced Glasgow's first Poet Laureate in autumn 1999, and was awarded the Queen's Gold Medal for Poetry in 2000. His website is at: www.edwinmorgan.com

Daniele Pantano is a poet, translator, and editor of Haerter, *M.A.G.*, and Niederngasse. He was born in Langenthal, Switzerland, of Sicilian and German parentage. An exile, he currently lives in Brandon, Florida, with his wife and their two children.

Clare E. Potter was born in South Wales. After three years in Mississippi studying an MA in Afro-Caribbean literature, she spent ten years teaching and writing in New Orleans. She won the John Tripp Award for Spoken Poetry in 2004 and her poetry collection, *Spilling Histories* will be published this year by Cinnamon Press. She has just started her PhD in creative writing at Cardiff University. Clare recently won a Future Focus on the Arts Award and is using the bursary to fund a trip to New Orleans to write a book of prose-poems about the impact of Katrina. Clare can be contacted by email: clare_potter_5@hotmail.com

David Radavich is the author of *Slain Species* (Court Poetry Press, London), *By the Way: Poems over the Years* (Buttonwood, 1998), and *Greatest Hits* (Pudding House, 2000). His plays have been performed across the U.S., including five Off-Off-Broadway productions, and in Europe. He also enjoys writing essays on poetry and drama.

Jay Ramsay is the author of many books including his New & Selected Poems *Kingdom of the Edge* (Element, 1999), *Alchemy—the art of transformation* (Thorsons, 1997: also available in Italian, Portuguese, Hebrew, German, and Dutch), *Tao Te Ching* with Martin Palmer (Element/Vega reprint 2002), his radical new book *Crucible of Love—the alchemy of passionate relationships* (O Books, 2005), and *The Heart's Ragged Evangelist* (PSAvalon, 2005).

Rochelle Ratner: books include two novels: *Bobby's Girl* (Coffee House Press, 1986) and *The Lion's Share* (Coffee House Press, 1991) and sixteen poetry books, including *House and Home* (Marsh Hawk Press, 2003) and *Beggars at the Wall* (Ikon, October 2005). An anthology she edited, *Bearing Life: Women's Writings on Childlessness*, was published in January 2000 by The Feminist Press. She lives in New York City where she teaches Creative Writing in alternative environments and reviews regularly for Library Journal. More information and links to her writing on the Internet can be found on her homepage: www.rochelleratner.com.

Ron Riddell, writer and peace-activist, is one of New Zealand's most widely published poets. Riddell has worked and performed in a number of countries, including Scotland, England, Chile, Colombia, El Salvador, Australia and the U.S.A., where his latest book, the award-winning collection, *Leaves of Light* was published in a bi-lingual edition (English/Spanish), in 2005. He has also been involved in a number of peace and cultural initiatives in Colombia, Chile, U.S.A., El Salvador and New Zealand. A painter, musician and the author of a number of plays and novels, he has published 15 collections of verse. At present, he lives in the New Zealand capital city, Wellington, where he is Director of The Wellington International Poetry Festival.

Dee Rimbaud is an artist, poet and novelist. He is author of two full-length poetry collections, *The Bad Seed* and *Dropping Ecstasy With The Angels*; and one novel, *Stealing Heaven From The Lips Of God*. As 2006 begins, he is frantically trying to redecorate his home to put it on the market and simultaneously editing and preparing the manuscript of *The Book Of Hopes And Dreams*. By the time it is published he anticipates he will be on the road somewhere in Europe with his partner, Su and daughter, Rosie Sunshine. His adventures will be recorded in his travel-blog: http://aaron-aardvark.blogspot.com/ His website is at: www.thunderburst.co.uk

Lori Romero is an editor and co-founder of Cezanne's Carrot . Her first chapbook, *Wall to Wall*, was published by Finishing Line Press. Her short story, "Strange Saints," was a semifinalist in the Sherwood Anderson Fiction Award, and her short screenplay won the Manhattan Short Film Festival's Scripts and Screenplay Competition. Her poetry and fiction have been published in over sixty journals and anthologies. She was nominated for a 2005 Pushcart Prize. For more information, see her website: www.tarecords.com/loriromero.html or email her; lori@tarecords.com

Lawrence Sail has published nine collections of poems, most recently *Eye-Baby* (Bloodaxe Books, 2006). In 2005 Enitharmon brought out a collection of his essays, *Cross-currents*. He has edited a number of anthologies, including *First and Always* (Faber, 1988) and (co-edited with Kevin Crossley-Holland) *The New Exeter Book of Riddles* (Enitharmon, 1999) and *Light Unlocked: Christmas Card Poems* (Enitharmon 2005). He has been chairman of The Arvon Foundation and Director of the Cheltenham Festival of Literature, and has frequently worked abroad for the British Council, ioncluding visits to Bosnia, Colombia, Egypt, India and Ukraine. In 2004 he received a Cholmondeley Award.

Lorraine Sautner, a resident of Fairfield County, Connecticut, is the Founder/Director of "Poets vs Poverty," a humanitarian arts organization that fights poverty "one word at a time" through poetry-related venues, including AEGIS magazine. Ms. Sautner enjoys reading and writing poetry with transcendental, spiritual, and romantic themes. She holds a master's degree in Library and Information Science; a bachelor's degree in English/Writing; and hopes to begin divinity school in late 2006. She also writes under the pen name Sterling Peony.

Maggie Sawkins lives in Southsea, Hampshire where she organises Tongues & Grooves poetry and music nights. She has been widely published, and a pamphlet collection, *Charcot's Pet*, is available from Flarestack Publishing. She is working on her first full collection, whose title, Dear Mr Popa, is in response to Vasko Popa's *The Little Box*. In 2004, she read at The Troubadour in London as one of their new summer voices. Maggie teaches at South Downs College near Portsmouth where she is also a mental health supports needs co-ordinator.

Myra Schneider: recent poetry books are *Insisting on Yellow*, new and selected poems, (Enitharmon, 2000), *Writing My Way Through Cancer*, a fleshed-out journal with poems (Jessica Kingsley 2003) and *Multiplying The Moon* (Enitharmon, 2004). She has co-edited three anthologies of women's poetry and a fourth, partly Arts Council funded, *Images of Women*, will be published in November 2006. She wrote the popular writing handbook: *Writing for Self-Discovery* (Element 1998) with John Killick. She is one of the Poetry School's core tutors.

Andrew Shelley: Poet/critic. Born 1962, West Yorkshire, England. Educated at Oxford and Cambridge, First Class Degree, Research Fellowship, Ph.D. on Samuel Beckett's later prose. Part-time teaching. Articles, poems and reviews in many magazines. Regular contributor to the English magazine *Tears in the Fence*. Previous publications include *Peaceworks* (The Many Press, 1996) and *Requiem Tree* (Spectacular Diseases, 2002). *Thornsongs* is a pamphlet of seven prose poems issued in the States by Unarmed in 2005 and distributed free.

Penelope Shuttle was born in Staines, Middlesex, in 1947. Since 1980 she has published six collections of poems, a Selected Poems (Poetry Book Society Recommendation, 1997, available from Carcanet), novels, and is co-author of two widely-read prose works, The Wise Wound and Alchemy for Women, dealing with the psychology and creative aspect of menstruation and its part in redefining the role and reality of women. Her work has been widely anthologised. Since 1970 she has lived in Falmouth, Cornwall.

K.V. Skene: poems have appeared in numerous Canadian, U.K., U.S., Irish and Australian publications Two chapbooks, *Only a Dragon* (2002) and *A Calendar of Rain* (2004), won the Shaunt Basmajian Chapbook Award (Canada). Another chapbook, *Edith* (a series of poems on Nurse Edith Cavell) was published by Flarestack Publishing in 2004. A book *Love in the (Irrational) Imperfect* is forthcoming from Hidden Brook Press (Canada). A long-term expat Canadian, K.V. Skene is presently living in Oxford.

Thomas R. Smith is a poet, essayist, editor, and teacher living in River Falls, Wisconsin. His books of poetry include Keeping the Star (New Rivers Press, 1988), Horse of Earth (Holy Cow! Press, 1994), The Dark Indigo Current (Holy Cow! Press, 2000), and Winter Hours (Red Dragonfly Press, 2005), as well as many chapbooks, most recently Peace Vigil: Poems for an Election Year (and After) (2004). His work was selected for The Best American Poetry 1999, the prestigious Scribner anthology. His work has appeared in the UK in Urthona and in Ireland in Poetry Ireland.

Jon Stallworthy was educated at Rugby School, in the Royal West African Frontier Force, and at Magdalen College, Oxford. His books include eight collections of poems, two critical studies of Yeats' poetry, *The Penguin Book of Love Poetry*, *The Fragments and War Poems*, and two biographies: *Wilfred Owen* (which won the Duff Cooper Memorial Prize, the W.H.Smith Literary Award, the E.M.Forster Award) and *Louis MacNeice* (which won the Southern Arts Literary Prize). More recently, he has published *Rounding the Horn: Collected Poems and Singing School*, 'the autobiography we would like all poets to write' (*Oxford Today*). Having been a Professor of English Literature at Cornell and Oxford, he is now a Senior Research Fellow of Wolfson College, Oxford, and a Fellow of the British Academy.

Anne Stevenson is the author of over a dozen volumes of poetry, including this year's *Granny Scarecrow, The Collected Poems, 1955-1995, Four and a Half Dancing Men,* and *Correspondences.* She is the author of several volumes of literary criticism as well, and also of the controversial *Bitter Fame: A Life of Sylvia Plath.* Stevenson was writer-in-residence at the University of Dundee, 1973-75, a fellow at Lady Margaret Hall, Oxford, 1975-77, and writer-in-residence at Bulmershe College, Reading, Berkshire, 1977-78, and the University of Edinburgh, 1987-89. She was also a Northern Arts Literary Fellow at Newcastle and Durham, 1981-82 and 1984-85.

Ray Succre has been writing with a profession in mind for about thirteen years. He began writing poetry as his primary work in 1997 and has also written several stageplays and collections of short stories. He began publishing August of 2004, and has been published in *Aesthetica, Poetry Salzburg Review, Poetry Nottingham,* and around fifty others both in the U.S. and abroad. He currently lives as a resident of southern coastal Oregon, U.S., with his loving wife Maisy, and his baby boy, Painter. He is between dishwashing jobs. More on Ray Succre can be found at his webpage: http://raysuccre.blogspot.com

Tricia Torrington lives in Cheltenham and has been published in a number of anthologies and magazines. She was one of two writers featured in "Rubin's Figure" in 1986. She is also a member of the Border Poets and recently edited and appeared in their latest anthology, "A Brush with Words", a joint venture with the Royal Academy Schools Alumni. She is married to the poet, Michael Henry.

Fiona Ritchie Walker is originally from Montrose, Angus in Scotland and now lives in Blaydon, near Newcastle. She has two poetry collections: *Lip Reading* (Diamond Twig) and *Garibaldi's Legs* (Iron Press). Her poetry also features in magazines and anthologies, including Virago/Writing Women's *Wild Cards,* the British Council/Picador *New Writing 11* and several anthologies from New Writing Scotland. Fiona's short stories have been published on literary websites and in *Newcastle Stories 1, Bracket* and *September Stories* (all Comma Press). In 2006, her story sequence will appear in *Ellipsis 2,* (Comma) together with stories by Anne Stevenson and Polly Clark.

Joanna M. Weston, born in England, lives in Western Canada; married, 3 sons, two cats. A writer, knitter, and gardener. Is a full-time writer of poetry, short-stories, children's books and poetry reviews. Has published internationally for many years online, in print journals and anthologies. Has a middle-reader, *The Willow-Tree Girl*, and a chapbook, *Watch-Night*, in print.

Jackie Wills has published three collections of poetry. Her first, Powder Tower, was shortlisted for the 1995 T.S.Eliot prize. The most recent is Fever Tree (Arc 2003). She's been a ghost writer and journalist. Her poetry's appeared on a dress by Helen Storey, paper napkins, on cafe walls, canvases and t shirts. She lives in Brighton. Some of her work can be read on:
http://jackiewillspoetry.blogspot.com/

Juliet Wilson is an Edinburgh based poet, reviewer and charity worker. Her poetry has been widely published and she has performed at various venues in Edinburgh. Her pamphlet 'Bougainvillea Dancing' sold out earlier this year, having raised over £200 for charities working in Malawi. Her website is at:
http://julietwilson.mysite.wandoo-members.co.uk and she has a blog of environmental poetry, crafts and reviews at
http://craftygreenpoet.blogspot.com.

Bohdan Yuri: Ukrainian/American writer living in Florida. *"Ukraina: Sons & Daughters"* c.1984 - a collection of short stories. *"The Letters"*, c. 1991 - (non-fiction). Has had poems published in various magazines such as; Niederngasse, Carillon, Thought, Panic, X Magazine, Rearview Quarterly, etc.